Gospel in Transformation

Lectures & Presentations at the Gossner Theological College

Gospel in Transformation

Rethinking of Gossner's Insights, Lutheran Heritage in relation to Mission

Ulrich Schoentube

Christian World Imprints™

&

Gossner Theological College

First Published in 2016 by

Christian World Imprints™
Christian Publishing & Books from India
H-12 Bali Nagar, **New Delhi-110015**
info@christianworldimprints.com
www.ChristianWorldImprints.com
Phone: +91 11 25465925

&

Gossner Theological College
Main Road, **Ranchi-834001**
gtcranchi@rediffmail.com
Phone: +91 651 2350005

ISBN: 978-93-5148-123-2 (HB)
ISBN: 978-93-5148-124-9 (PB)

Printed in India.

Foreword

'Gospel in Transformation' is an inspiring collection of addresses and articles authored and presented on different occasions by Rev. Dr. Ulrich Schoentube. During the period of 7 years, he was the Mission Director of Gossner Mission, Berlin. Dr. Ulrich, as a young, energetic, enthusiastic and cheerful Missions Director travelled widely and at regular intervals, in the mission area and identified himself with the locals as a fellow worker. As a member of the Brass Band Team, he became easily approachable and accessible to a great number of leaders and workers. I had the opportunity to see him in action during his mission visits and conference deliberations in India and also in his current parish work in Germany and therefore I am pleased to write this foreword.

Dr. Ulrich divides the compilation into 4 sections with a concluding contribution covering the focal areas, namely, 'Biographical Sketches', the 'Lutheran Heritage', 'Social Freedom', and the 'Ecumenical Approaches'.

The author made an investigative research into the life, service and mission of Johannes Evangelista Gossner, the founder of the Mission. He brought into this publication, the various insights of Father Gossner, his passion for preaching the word of God, training of missionaries for ministries overseas, his impact over the lives of the peer groups and the contemporaries, his writings, his love for music and his role in deepening the worship services and not the least, what his associates spoke about him.

Prayer is said to be part of the personality of Fr. Gossner on the strength of which he was able to send out missionaries across the continents. India is uniquely privileged as one of the countries that came under the focus of the ministry of Gossner. The author also was able to present first hand knowledge of his experiences with the Gossner Church in Chotanagpur and was able to bring into light the early beginnings of Gossner missionaries, the hardships they had to withstand, the disappointments they suffered and how Fr. Gossner reiterated the fact that preaching of the word was the task for the missionaries and conversion is the work of the Holy Spirit as such; preaching the word to the time of judgment of the people is what matters and the conversion does not. The author also investigates the struggles of the Adivasis, their hopes and aspirations for the intervention of the missionaries to mitigate their suffering from the shackles of poverty and the caste system and not to speak of the oppressive regimes. The dominance of the Kings, the Zamindars and the Jagirdars; their irrational taxation; social and land rights deprivations on one hand and the Lutheran theory of accepting authorities as those coming from God and the incompatibility of measures to oppose the State authorities on the other; often, left the people and the passionate missionaries in a dilemma.

The comparative study of the author, made between Johann Hinrich Wichern and Johannes Evangelista Gossner; Birsa Munda and Thomas Muentzer were quite revealing as to how the perceptions were held and peoples struggles were tackled by the early church fathers and their contemporaries in the State and the Society. Gossner's conviction that it is the training of the heart of the man that qualifies one to be a preacher or a missionary as opposed to the theory of training of mind, qualifying one to be the preacher or the missionary.

The author also brings the insights of early conversions, breaking of caste barriers, the in-house difficulties within the rank and file of the missionaries, denominational polarization and such other.

Dr. Schoentube makes a timely reminder of the contentions of Martin Luther, the Father of Reformation, and that of Carlstadt, that pictures, images, statues and the like tempt humans to idol-worship reaffirming the fact that all honour and glory belong solely to God. Human as we are, with a high degree of vulnerability, it is helpful to be reminded of this fact so that, we do go after the creator God and not His creatures.

The author makes a strong and a positive observation about the forms of worship that was brought from foreign land and planted in the local soil, resulting in unintended deprivations of the local culture, the language and the ethos. This is not just a phenomenon of Gossner Missionaries and the Gossner Church but, a universal fact that these forms of worship went on and on, without realizing the relevance and the unintended effects of such worship and liturgical practices.

The author, in the chapter on 'Ecumenical Approaches' ably articulates the deliberations of the World Council of Churches Assemblies, the Mission Conferences, specially Edinburgh 2010 and makes a strong case for tolerance and greater understanding of the varying denominations and even non-believers; warranting space to listen to their contention as part of the new discoveries of the Grace and Power of God. This in effect gives one, a new strength of faith, to face a new age and a new task with a new consecration. The GELC's inter-religious prayer observance was found to be trend setting for the traditional missionaries. This resulted in a new way of understanding the people of different faiths.

Dr. Ulrich's reflections are thought provoking and faith strengthening. The Gospel, wherever preached and practiced proved to be a great transformational experience; therefore, it is not developing a christian culture but Gospel entering into every culture for its redeeming power, lest the unreached perish but be blessed to the eternity. Dr. Schoentube drove home the inner message of early missionary fathers like Fr. Gossner - their own search for salvation and the urgency with which they toiled to ensure that the Gospel of

Jesus that grants the gift of forgiveness, the promise of salvation for every repenting soul of the humankind becomes accessible.

I have, therefore, great pleasure to commend the book as a 'must read'.

Dr. Oliver Jetti
Chancellor – SHIATS University, and
President – Church History Association of India

Contents

Remember those who led you, who spoke the word of God to you; and considering the result of their conduct, imitate their faith. Jesus Christ is the same yesterday and today and forever.
Hebr.13:7-8.

Introduction

The verse from the Letter to the Hebrews, quoted often by Johannes Evangelista Gossner (1773-1858), can be seen in Berlin wherever Gossner had an influence. It is written on a board in the Elisabeth Clinic, which Gossner founded. It is cited on his grave in the "Friedhof am Halleschen Tor" cemetery. Finally, it is engraved in a threshold at the former place of the Mission House in Berlin Friedenau, built by Gossner's successor, Karl Plath (1829-1901). The Bible verse from the Letter to the Hebrews characterises Gossner's belief that Christ is an immutable word of God, shaping the heart of an individual and the world. That is God's Mission. Gossner made here no separation between the oversea and inner mission – the communication of the Gospel as a proclamation all around the world and as the work of social welfare within his own community.[1]

1 Since the time of Johann Hinrich Wichern it was common in Germany to differ between "Innere (engl. inner) Mission" and "Äussere (engl. external) Mission". The "Innere Mission" covers the Church social service to the

In this spirit, Gossner sent out his missionaries to various regions of the world in the 19th century. Their impact in the Chotanagpur region, in today's modern Jharkhand, amongst the Adivasi, the indigenous people of India, was particularly prolific. In their work, the missionaries saw, how the Gospel that they wished to impart underwent many different transformational processes. "Remember those who led you" (Heb.13:7)! How can such transformational processes be described if the Gospel is brought to another cultural area and what happens during this kind of "inculturation"?

We credit Theo Sundermeier for bringing a new understanding of these different processes of communication of the Christian faith to the missiology debate. He assumes that the biblical texts should be understood as open systems of communication, in the meaning of the concept of Umberto Eco's "Open Work". In addition, Sundermeier's work is characterised by the dialogical philosophy of the Jewish philosopher Emanuel Lévinas, who sees the "I" as first being constituted ontologically through the "Other". Based on both inspirations, Sundermeier comprehends the communication of biblical texts to another cultural context in a specific way. Thus, the message of a text is firstly revealed in the listener as a subject, in his comprehension and in his reception. The listener is changed but also the message, which is heard in a specific way that is coloured by pre-existing cultural conditions. "The message is changed in its very understanding."[2] Via this type of cultural acceptance new horizons for the Gospel will be revealed, which were initially unrecognisable.

---

needy in the Church's home country or home context, otherwise it is called "Diakonie" = Diaconate. The "Äussere Mission" means the propagation of the Gospel abroad. We use for the difference here the terms "inner mission" and "oversea mission". For the difference see also the article in this book: " … and covered me with kisses …" – Johann Hinrich Wichern (1808-1881) visiting Johannes Evangelista Gossner (1773-1858) in Berlin.

2 Theo Sundermeyer, Begegnung mit dem Fremden, Plädoyer für eine verstehende Missionswissenschaft, in: Theo Sundermeyer, Konvivenz und Differenz, Studien zu einer verstehenden Missionswissenschaft. Anlässlich seines 60. Geburtstages herausgegeben von Volker Küster, Erlangen 1995, p. 80.

Only in these transfer processes in another culture, the fullness of the message of the Gospel is able to blossom. "To understand the meaning of the Gospel, we need different cultures, since it is only here that it can achieve its objective."[3] At another place, Sundermayer understands this transfer process as inculturation according to Phil. 2.16 christologically as a kenotic process. Christ becomes flesh in another culture. And this happens in the process: "It is not only the missionary that changes, however, but also the church that has sent him. The culture in which the Gospel is incarnated is also transformed by it. Finally, the message itself is changed".[4]

In his theory, Sundermeier interprets inculturation as incarnation. He instructs that such transfer processes of the Gospel to another cultural form or context should not be interpreted in the sense of linear dependencies, for example, as a Gospel path that runs in a line from North to South. There are no "senders" and no subordinate "recipients" of the messages. Instead, the recipient is the subject of the understanding and appropriation of the message in its specific cultural format. An equal hermeneutical dialogue on biblical texts between the various theologies of the world is thereby facilitated. This way of thinking and its practical consequences have still not arrived in our churches, which is why we should with Sundermeier take every opportunity to point out the following: We are always Christians in the face of and in dialogue with the Other.

Nevertheless we might question, whether this theory does not actually roll the biblical text and the message it contains into one. Does the specific cultural communication of a biblical text truly lead to a different or to a modified message? And if the message changes as part of the transfer process, why can we then assume that

3 Theo Sundermeyer, Begegnung mit dem Fremden, Plädoyer für eine verstehende Missionswissenschaft, in: Theo Sundermeyer, Konvivenz und Differenz, Studien zu einer verstehenden Missionswissenschaft. Anlässlich seines 60. Geburtstages herausgegeben von Volker Küster, Erlangen 1995, p. 80.

4 Theo Sundermeyer, Inkulturation als Entäußerung, in: Jan A. B. Jongeneel u.a. Mission and Ecumenism. Essays in Intercultural Theology, Frankfurt/Main 1992, p. 213.

this is the same Gospel, the same Christ in his identity throughout different times and cultures (Heb. 13:8)? According to the theory do we understand Christianity as a world religion that is identical with itself, or more as "Christianities" - as more or less related religious worldviews within different cultures?

These questions should not dismiss Sundermeier's theory. However, they outline a problematic area, in which the debate around the inculturation of the Gospel is held. It is clear that these transfer processes and mutual influences are not unidirectional linear processes but instead are complex hermeneutical processes in the search of truth within different cultural contexts. However, it is theologically critical to note that in this concept, the intention to avoid any superiority between "missionary" and "recipient" lead to an understanding to declare the recipient, the subject of the message, in its dimension to reveal the truth: the recipient himself transforms the message by his very process of understanding. On the contrary: When the term incarnation is used – this has been picked up extremely prolifically in African theology[5] – one can state the following: the human subject does not appropriate the truth of faith, but it is revealed by the word of God in His mission. In other words, both the "missionary" and the "recipient" receive the truth of the Christian faith via God. The individual is not the subject of the message rather it is God sending the message. This truth is in various cultures and times; it provides the one and the same message of the love of God for His people, which is shown in crucifixion and resurrection of Jesus Christ. In my opinion the substance of this "message" remains the same, whilst it assumes different forms in various cultures and periods. For this reason, I feel that inculturation can be fully understood as incarnation in this sense, namely that the message of the Gospel is existing in an ongoing process of becoming different forms in the world, in different cultures and at different times. The Gospel is in transformation and this is the only way of its existence, whereby its fullness can only be appropriated with every new transformation and will be completed in the eschaton.

5 Kwame Bediako, Christianity in Africa, The Renewal of a Non-Western Religion, Edinburgh 1995.

The present study of mission-history traces this diverse process of transformation of the shape of the Gospel using an example of a region in North-East India. The contributions and articles are exploratory attempts to describe the transformations of the Gospel.

These sketches are lectures, held between 2007 and 2014 at the Gossner Theological College in Ranchi. On the occasion of every partnership visit, the college compiled academic evenings under the guidance of Principal Dr. Manmasih Ekka, in which we discussed the present studies, which the college had requested for the most part.

The lectures dealing with the history of the Christian missions are not listed in their original chronological order here. The classification of the lectures intends here to emulate the transformation of the Gospel. In this respect, the articles and contributions have been split into four sections.

The first section, "Biographical Sketches", contains biographical studies of the founder of the mission. Johannes Evangelista Gossner is the shared founding figure of the worldwide Gossner family and namesake of the Gossner-Church. In particular the path of the "Heart of Man" (Herzbüchlein) depicts the transformational process of the Gospel using different cultures and times. Gossner himself is not the starting point but his "Heart of Man" is woven into a much longer tradition spreading the Gospel by using images in its respective different cultural flavours.

The second section, "Lutheran Heritage", discusses the Lutheran roots of this branch of God's mission. In this section, there is an article on the liturgy of Gossner Church that keenly shows how an agenda, which originally functioned as a compromise between Reformed and Lutherans, became in the cultural transformation in Indian context of Gossner Church, a symbol of Lutheran identity.

The third section, "Social Freedom", turns its attention to the largest field of learning for the German missionaries with the Adivasi in the transformational process of the Gospel. The missionaries grew in their understanding of the social relevance of the Gospel. This section begins with the story of the very first conversion, which already reveals a different cultural understanding of the Gospel amongst the Oraon-Adivasi than that of the missionaries – "Mission as misunderstanding". This learning process of recognising the Gospel within its social context accompanied the missionaries in their attitude towards traditional land legislation and in conflict with new laws – a subject that is unfortunately a topical one, even today. For those readers interested in the history of the Christian missions, the evaluation of the German sources is interesting, because they are hard to access in India.

The fourth section is dedicated to the current ecumenical debates. Here, the challenges have to be named in the reflection on the legacy of the Edinburgh Mission Conference of 1910 and on the Mission Statement of the 10th General Assembly of the World Council of Churches in Busan "Mission in Changing Landscapes". Finally, the emphasis is placed on the last contribution – "Tolerance and Mission". This article describes a specific Lutheran perspective beyond the cultural transformation of the Gospel, namely to define the belief in its dimension of revealing the truth as a gift, which enables tolerant and respectful dealings with other faiths and religions in a very special way.

A retrospective by Principal Dr. Ekka, who takes a look back over the academic evenings and discussions, ends the publication.

The studies would never be realized without the support of my wife and the fruitful discussions and exchange of opinions within the Gossner family. I would like to give special thanks to Dr. Klaus Roeber, Dr. Klaus von Stieglitz, Principal Dr. Manmasih Ekka, Rev. Idan Topno, Bishop Dr. CSR Topno, Moderator Dr. Nelson Lakra, Rev. T.S. Cyril Hans and Rev. Dr. C. Sumit A. Kerketta. Dr. Volker Waffenschmidt. All these esteemed personalities provided me help and support in enabling me to focus on my thoughts and in linguistic interpretation and translation of many articles. I am also grateful to Rev. Lisa Smith and Jane Tournee for their translation assistance.

Quid enim habes, quod non accipisti!
1 Cor.4:7

Dr. Ulrich Schoentube

Section 1

Biographical Sketches

1. Johannes Evangelista Gossner

1.1 Who was Gossner? - His contemporaries recount

Amalie Sieveking: Gossner – a pious man

"The 'Christ in us', his favourite thought and concept, shines so brightly from his entire being that any personal dealings with him provide the best commentary on his writings. Always composed, with his soul forever focused in one direction – to exude love and kindness, and in his presence one feels as if in a sanctuary, even when he does not utter a single word. In mixed society, he spoke little and often seemed reserved. He does not enjoy the futile debate of spiritual matters, but if he notices that an individual is truly interested of spiritual nourishment, then no other person is more prepared to help that individual to heal than he is."[6]

Johann Hinrich Wichern: Gossner – an opinionated contemporary

"In the evening I went to see Gossner. I entered his house with great joy. His Missionary activities have always appealed to me, more than anything else. He lives in a pleasant summer-

6 Emma Poel, Denkwürdigkeiten aus dem Leben von Amalie Sieveking, in deren Auftrage von einer Freundin derselben verfasst, Hamburg 1860; Johann Hinrich Wichern, Beiblatt der Fliegenden Blätter aus dem Rauhen Hause 10 (1859), No. 11, p. 172. The quotation from Sieveking's biography can also be found in: Hermann Dalton, Johannes Gossner. Ein Lebensbild aus der Kirche des 19. Jahrhunderts, Berlin 1874, p. 271 (Transl. U.S.).

house, with many flowers blooming in front of it. This is where we sat down. ...

A few minutes later we were having a lively debate - in which on several occasions I was at the point of picking up my hat and stick and leaving for ever. I cannot deny it; I have almost never seen a man who I otherwise find to be so honourable become so rude and so arrogant so very quickly. ... Soon we were called in to tea. Afterwards I left. But he tried to be alone with me, hugged me and covered me with kisses ... and asked me to visit him again."[7]

Carl Büchsel: Gossner – A man of prayer

Seldom have I found someone who could pray like old Gossner did. He well prayed for the walls of the hospital, he well prayed for the hearts of the sisters working at the hospital, he well prayed for the hearts of the rich, who thereupon donated generously far beyond the boundaries of our native country, he well prayed for the mission station in India and he did pray well on earth. By his prayer he strengthened and supported the hearts of the missionaries against temptation and threat, and by his prayer enriched the works and accompanied them far into the world. Not only here at his grave are his spiritual children standing, but his children were spread wide beyond our native country. A praying man old Gossner was.[8]

7 Johann Hinrich Wichern, Gesammelte Schriften D. Johann Hinrich Wicherns. Briefe und Tagebuchblätter D. Johann Hinrich Wicherns, I. Band 1826-1848, Hamburg 1901, p. 266 (Transl. U.S.).

8 Johann Dettloff Prochnow, Johannes Evangelista Gossner, nebst Übersicht der Gossnerschen Missionstätigkeit, Berlin 1859, p. 81 (Transl. by Jörg Schneider).

1.2 Who was Gossner? – Truth and fiction: Biography

There is a gap in the biographical tradition for Gossner.The first biographer was Johann Dettloff Prochnow[9], one of the India missionaries, who later would become inspector of the Gossner mission.[10] He edited a two-part biography, which mainly consisted of diaries and letters. Unfortunately the second part ended as early as 1826. Starting with this point onwards begins from a biographical perspective the period of major interest for us, actually Gossner's time in the Berlin revival movement, when the visible works of the inner and oversea mission arise. This gap was extremely difficult to close in the subsequent biographies by Hermann Dalton[11], Walter Holsten[12] and Hans Lokies[13] and even in Charlotte Sauer's novel.[14] Presumably Prochnow had retained the majority of Gossner's detailed diary entries and letters for the publication of the second main part of Gossner's biography. In addition, the Gossner Mission Archive suffered major damage during the war. As biographical details regarding the second half of Gossner's life can only be derived from originals with great difficulty, we can only listen to the stories of his followers. We can

9 Karl Foertsch, Dr. Dettloff Prochnow, Gossners Missionar und Nachfolger, Berlin 1939.

10 Johann Dettloff Prochnow, Johannes Gossner. Biographie aus Tagebüchern und Briefen, Erster Theil bis zum Schluß seiner Wirksamkeit in Petersburg, Berlin o.J.; Johann Dettloff Prochnow: Johannes Gossner. Biographie aus Tagebüchern und Briefen. Zweiter Theil bis zu seinem Tode, Berlin 1874.

11 Hermann Dalton, Johannes Gossner. Ein Lebensbild aus der Kirche des 19. Jahrhunderts, Berlin 1874.

12 Walter Holsten, Johannes Evangelista Gossner. Glaube und Gemeinde, Göttingen 1949. Holsten describes mainly the development of the external missions to Australia, Papua, India etc. He publishes his book after World War II. However, during his research he was still able to access the archive, which was complete at the time. As most of the archived material was destroyed by fire, Holsten's work has the status of a primary source.

13 Hans Lokies, Johannes Gossner. Ein Bekenner und Diener Jesu Christi. Zeugen des gegenwärtigen Gottes, 2nd Ed., Gießen 1956.

14 Charlotte Sauer, Fremdling und Bürger, Lebensbild des Johannes Evangelista Gossner, Berlin 1967.

feel the spirit and imagine the impact of Gossner's person and at the same time we are forced to accept and acknowledge the limits of historical objectivity.

Gossner was born in 1773 in a Hausen in Swabia. After attending school in Waldstaetten and Augsburg, Gossner then studies at the Catholic theological seminary in Ingolstadt. He becomes a priest. As a young chaplain he admires the great preachers of the Catholic revival movement Johann Michael Sailer and Martin Boos. The ecclesiastical authorities find this so suspicious that in 1802 Gossner was taken into custody for priests in Göggingen. After his rehabilitation Gossner takes over a pastorate in Dirlewang, an important point in his life. It is here that he employs Ida Maria Bauberger as his housekeeper, who would go on to accompany him as far as Berlin. And it was also here that he wrote his bestseller, the 'Herzbüchlein' (Heart of Man).[15] It was still being translated into 50 languages in Gossner's lifetime. Following further posts as secretary of the inter-denominational fellowship the Basel Christian Society (Baseler Christenthumsgesellschaft), at the Frauenkirche in Munich and as a teacher of religious education in Dusseldorf, his path led him to St. Petersburg. In 1820, Gossner was called by the Russian Tsar Alexander I to the post of pastor at the Catholic Maltese Church. The Tsar planned to initiate a spiritual revival in Russia. The parish in St. Petersburg was Gossner's great love. This is apparent in a hymnbook, which contained the famous "Bless and protect us" for the very first time[16] and a book of daily devotions,

15 Johannes Evangelista Gossner, Das Herz des Menschen. Ein Tempel Gottes oder eine Werkstätte des Satans, Berlin 1812. (engl ed.: The Heart of Man. Either a temple of God or the habitation of Satan, Pa 1822). See also the article "Gossner's 'Heart of Man' – origin and reception" in this book.

16 Johannes Evangelista Gossner, Sammlung auserlesener Lieder von der erlösenden Liebe, Leipzig 1825. Gossner understood the song, which was very often handed down as a nursery rhyme and versified according to the priestly blessing (Num. 6, 24-26), as a liturgical antiphony between liturgy and the congregation. Consequently it can be found in the book under section XXIII. Antiphonies (No. 774). It is noteworthy that the various known versions of the third verse "Amen, Amen, Amen, praise be to all the names of our Lord

the "Schatzkaestchen" (The Spiritual Casked).[17] As part of the Holy Alliance, the Tsar came under the influence of Prince Metternich, on whose recommendation Gossner was expelled from St. Petersburg.[18] Although Gossner personally experienced the despotism of state authority, but he saw in general in authority a tool of God's will, which is clear from the foreword to the "Schatzkaestchen".[19] Later on in 1848 this would lead him to take sides with the Prussian king and to write the following in a pamphlet: "Whoever still has a heart for 'justice and law', then pray for the king. ... The enemies (the social democrats) have only the Devil on their side."[20] – This was also Gossner.

After leaving St. Petersburg, a period began in Gossner's life, which his biographer describes as "unstable and volatile".[21] Gossner

---

Jesus Christ, who is the first and last." and "Amen, Amen, Amen, praise and honour to the name of Jesus Christ our Lord, for He loves to bless us so!" are not originally part of Gossner's song of blessing. They can both be found in the song "Jesus Christ give us strength", which is reprinted after Gossner's song of praise in the hymn book (no. 775).

17 Johannes Gossner, Schatzkästchen enthaltend biblische Betrachtungen mit erbaulichen Liedern auf alle Tage im Jahre zur Beförderung häuslicher Andacht und Gottseligkeit, Leipzig 1825. English Edition: Johannes Gossner, The Spiritual Casket of daily Bible Meditations ... Translated from the German. With an introduction by ... E. H. Bickersteth, London 1864.

18 Tsar Alexander was the original instigator the "Holy Alliance" between Russia, Austria and Prussia. If the tsar's motivation behind the brotherhood of nations was a religious one, the Austrian minister von Metternich, however, was able to interpret this Holy Alliance as a binding league of ruling powers for the purpose of maintaining the monarchy. Thus, there was an influence on the tsar, who subsequently ordered the expulsion of the freemasons and awakened church groups, as Metternich was able to convince him of their links with revolutionary groups.

19 Johannes Gossner, Schatzkästchen (Spriritual Casket), preface: "I wish to honour and know the honouring of the authority of the state with no less loyalty or conscientiousness than I would give to loving God and my brothers with all my heart and to accord every man respect."

20 Festschrift zum 75-jährigen Bestehen der Gossnerschen Mission, Berlin 1911, p. 13f.

21 Hermann Dalton, Johannes Gossner, p. 259.

found acceptance in various estates in East Prussia, Pomerania and Silesia. Finally on 23rd July 1826 after much hesitation he converted in Königshain nearby Görlitz. Gossner applied for recognition of his theological qualifications at the Royal Consistory in Berlin and at the age of 54 he was required to repeat all examinations. For a probationary period he was assigned a pastoral position at the Sophienkirche (Saint Sophia's Church) in front of the Hamburger Tor and at the Luisenstadt Church. Finally in 1829, he was given the pastorate of the Lutheran branch of the Bethlehem Church Parish, a migrant parish of the Bohemian Brethren. This role finally combines his prolific and valuable impact on social welfare and in the external mission. Gossner founded kindergarten schools, which were the archetypes for Wichern charitable actions later on. From parish patient visitor associations he established the first evangelical hospital, which was inaugurated in 1837 in front of the Potsdam Gate. With respect to his oversea mission Gossner did not at first take an obvious step namely to participate in the mission school, which his predecessor, Johannes Jaenicke, had founded. This role was subsequently assumed by Jaenicke's son-in-law Johann Wilhelm Rückert,[22] who held it until 1849.[23] It is said that Rückert was difficult to work with, thus in 1831 Gossner followed the call of the "Comité der Gesellschaft zur Beförderung der Evangelischen Mission unter den Heiden" (Committee of the Society for the Promotion of the Evangelical Mission to the Heathens), later called Berlin Mission, which was set up in 1824. He led the Committee meetings in such a lively manner that it usually followed his advice, as Julius Richter

22 Hans J. Reichhardt, Die Böhmen in Berlin 1732-1982, p. 114. Rückert is known as the last Bohemian speaking preacher of the Lutheran community. However, there is no mention of him in the Church Registry. Otto Fischer, Evangelisches Pfarrerbuch für die Mark Brandenburg seit der Reformation, Berlin 1941, Vol. 1, p. 21.

23 Karl Friedrich Ledderhose, Johann Jänicke, der evangelisch Lutherische Prediger an der böhmischen – oder Bethlehems-Kirche zu Berlin, nach seinem Leben und Wirken, Berlin 1863, p. 104.

shows using the minutes of the meetings.[24] For the third anniversary of the young society in 1833, Gossner delivered a sermon from Schleiermacher's pulpit in the Church of the Holy Trinity[25], which since Dalton has been referred time and again as "his program".[26] On the occasion of this anniversary the society sent trained missionaries out to Africa for the very first time. This action provoked vigorous disputes. Gossner made sure that a certain August Gebel, whom he thought to be a "scoundrel"[27], was not sent as head of the group. Gebel was an educated theologist. However, this was a decisive factor for the committee. But this first mission failed after Gebel absconded in South Africa and Gossner felt that his opinion had indeed been validated, that scientific education for the training and sending of missionaries was not necessary, but a spiritual formation of the heart. Serious disagreement would follow when the purchase of a missionary house was completed. Gossner believed that the money would be better invested in missions to the tribals. Hence, in 1836 he left the committee with a crash, because of deep disagreement regarding the education of the candidates and the investment in to a Mission house. In the period that followed Gossner apparently tried to "abstain in every respect with the external mission work", as he writes in the "Biene auf dem Missionsfelde" (The Bee in the Mission Field), his missionary magazine, which he founded in 1834.[28]

He then received a letter from a "respectable gentleman in the city", offering him eight young men for training, who had been rejected by the Berlin Mission. As an aside, it was mentioned that this

24 Julius Richter, Geschichte der Berliner Missionsgesellschaft 1824-1924, Berlin 1924, p. 25.

25 Johannes Gossner, Missionspredigt. Delivered at the anniversary celebration of the mission society at the Church of the Holy Trinity in Berlin, Berlin on 29th May 1833, in: Johannes Gossner, Sammlung gedruckter und ungedruckter Predigten, Nürnberg 1838, pp. 549-585.

26 Herrmann Dalton, Johannes Gossner, p. 370. Hans Lokies: Johannes Gossner, Ein Bekenner und Diener Jesu Christi, p. 71.

27 Julius Richter, Geschichte der Berliner Missionsgesellschaft, p. 25.

28 Die Biene auf dem Missionsfelde 1837/ 5, p. 34 ("The Bee in the Mission Field", hereafter abbreviated to: Biene).

"respectable gentleman" was probably a certain Gottfried Wilhelm Lehmann, who belonged to the Baptist Free Church, which at the time was still banned in Prussia.[29] In his letter Lehmann recommends the eight young men Gossner for training for missionary service.[30] On the basis of this letter, Gossner invited the young men to meet with him. Gossner's diary contains details of this meeting. It was on 12th December 1836, at eight in the morning, when six of the eight young men as indicated arrived. This was probably an "unholy hour" for Gossner, as we would say today. Gossner actually adds in his diary above the time later: "early". The rest of the story has been recounted frequently. Gossner prays with the young men and realises that "not all of these men are actually awakened, at least for the most part."[31] He starts his own missionary training and sends his first missionaries out to Australia in cooperation with the Scottish Church Mission. Until his death in 1858 Gossner sent out 141 missionaries. These were predominantly craftsmen. Many went to India, where as early as 1919 an independent Lutheran church was founded for the indigenous people, the Adivasi. There is today among the historians an agreement that the success of the missionaries amongst the Adivasi was down to the very fact that they were craftsmen, in other words, they bore witness to the Gospel with both hands and heart.[32] However, India

29 Hans Luckey, Gottfried Wilhelm Lehmann und die Entstehung einer deutschen Freikirche, Kassel 1939, pp. 30-34. Lehmann was a pioneer of religious freedom outside of the main denominations. The fact that Gossner never mentions this key personality during this time, nor in the period that followed until his death, as far as known, would lead us to suspect, however, that he was endowed with a great deal more diplomacy than we tend to give his eccentric nature credit for. For he was a Lutheran with a Catholic background and understood only too well that his work was of course the work of the Lord, but that it was by promoted by worldly favour.

30 The letter is reproduced by Hermann Dalton, Johann Evangelista Gossner, p. 375.

31 The Gossner Mission Archive, G1-812, Personalakten des Stifters Johannes Evangelista Gossner 1828-1839, "Trennung von der Jänickeschen Mission, der älteren Berliner und Beginn einer eigenen Mission".

32 Joseph Bara, Unlocking Tribal Knowledge to the World: German Missionaries in Chhotanagpur, East India (1850-1930), in: Ulrich von der Heyden

was not the only location to which Gossner sent his missionaries, but with the support of other German, English or Dutch missionary groups they were also sent to Papua New Guinea, the Chattam Islands, or even to Greenland. With the first missionaries begins the history of the mission society, which was still in Gossner's lifetime in 1842 established and finally authorised by the King of Prussia as "Evangelischer Missionsverein zur Ausbreitung des Christenthums unter den Eingeborenen der Heidenlaender" (Evangelical Mission Society for the Propagation of Christianity amongst the Indigenous People of the Tribal Lands).[33]

When Gossner died in 1858, a long procession followed his coffin. At his grave, today the cemetery "Friedhof am Halleschen Tor", the erstwhile General Superintendent Carl Büchsel gave a moving eulogy. Büchsel said, the prayer was the centre of Gossners personality and his impact to the mission (see he quotation above).

1.3 Who was Gossner? – The main mission-theological perspectives

Gossner believed that mission is not a particularly special task, which should be the remit of the trained theologist or of a city missionary, but it is instead an integral duty of the entire church and of every single Christian. In his famous mission sermon, which he held when the first Berlin missionaries were sent in 1831, he said:

> "I therefore affirm: evangelical missions, or the preaching of the Gospel to all nations and at all times, and thus the sending forth of evangelical preachers to all nations and at all times, for the planting and dissemination of Christianity, for the happiness of the nations, of our fellow man and our brothers, who have also been redeeming, is the task

---

et al., Missionsgeschichte als Geschichte der Globalisierung von Wissen: transkulturelle Wissensaneignung in Afrika und Asien im 17, 18 and 19. Jahrhundert, Berlin 2010, p. 55: "Against this, the German missionaries could, with their down-to-earth approach and humanitarian dealing, win the heart of the tribal masses."

33 Walter Holsten, Johannes Evangelista Gossner, p. 386f.

> which is the most indispensable and based in the nature of Christianity, and at the same time, the most blessed and most gratifying business, the holiest and most important duty, which every Christian, and the entire Church, should make their own".[34]

This powerful sentence, which was used as the foundation of the sermon that followed, has an air of inspiration and impetus: everyone "should" (!) be a missionary. An apostolic understanding of the mission is important here, which has a Christological basis, as inspired by the Allgäu revivalist movement. Gossner's starting point is the fellowship of Christ in the heart of the individual. He already gives examples of this in his early work, his "Herzbüchlein" (Heart of Man). Accordingly all negative struggles of the heart such as envy and greed, etc., are eliminated when Christ enters the heart with his love and forgiveness. The substance of the heart is transformed by its communion with Christ. The personal union with Christ constitutes the foundation of the missionary's existence.[35] For this reason, a theological study is not a prerequisite to become a missionary but instead this union in the heart with Christ is most essential. Every single individual whose heart has been shaped by Christ is therefore a missionary. This leads to a second thought: the missionary, shaped in his heart by the communion with Christ, is an ambassador of Christ, as Christ himself was an ambassador of God's love. The core of understanding of the mission work is based in corresponding relationships: Just as the father sent Christ, so Christ sends the missionary. Gossner explains this in his mission sermon (as mentioned):

---

34 Johannes Evangelista Gossner, Missionspredigt, in: Johannes E. Gossner, Sammlung gedruckter und ungedruckter Predigten, p. 552. Hans Lokies, Johannes Gossner, p. 71 (Transl. U.S.). Lokies repeats different variants of this key sentence for the understanding of Gossner's mission work in his readworthy book.

35 Walter Holsten: Johann Evangelista Gossner, p. 28.

> "... a messenger of Christ must be sent by Christ, as Christ himself was sent by the Father, and must not go the tribes if sent forth by himself alone, he must not ... be sent forth by persons. ... Whoever has not been touched by Christ or anointed with the Holy Spirit, whoever has not been chosen, called and sent forth in this manner, such person should stay at home." [36]

What exactly does this communion with Christ mean? For Gossner, it was impossible to speak of Christ and his redemption without mentioning the "Christ in us": "... since Christ, who was crucified for us, cannot help us if he is not also alive in us."[37] In the first instance this signified that the life of Christ should be "viewed as example".[38] However, this also meant in the whole life seeking this fellowship with Christ within one's heart, and perceiving to the proximity and the distance of a deep and trusting faith and in both to know that one is held in God's hands. It is reported that Gossner himself use to speak in this way of faith right until his death. His followers pass on as his final and most important words: "My lambs! Jesus Christ, now all is well, now I am completely went out, there is no longer a yarn with me!"[39] This is the deep path of faith walked by Gossner. Until his very end he looked for the "*Christ in us*", who steps into place of the identity of the ego. It is only this internal interplay of the proximity and distance of personal belief, which leads to the inner and oversea mission of action, towards both the

---

36 Johannes Evangelista Gossner: Missionspredigt, p. 553 (Transl. U.S.).

37 Johannes Evangelista Gossner, Das Wachstum Christi in den Christen. Predigt am 1. Sonntag nach Epiphanias 1836, in: Johannes Gossner, Predigten, p. 709.

38 Ibid., p. 709: "If someone looks only at Christ and his death as a sacrifice for his sins, to console oneselves for fear of death and fear of hell, and not looking at HIM in his life as an example to be sanctified by him and be similar with him ... the one divides Christ, he has only half the Christ, and therefore no Christ, because the Christ crucified for us, does not help us if he does not live in us. Gal.2:20."

39 Hermann Dalton, Johannes Gossner, p. 425.

wretched souls at our door and the wretched souls far away – to the "Christ for us". For Gossner, the two went hand in hand, namely, the search for Christ inside of us and at the same time, witnessing the "Christ for us" in effective charitable actions. This is a continuous thread throughout Gossner's theology.

> "The more closer an individual lives in communion with Christ, more clearer will become his task as service to the world. The more we struggle with political and social justice, the more we need the strength of God's mercy... Wherever our starting point, the end result is the unity, which we all require. We can say: the personal and the global, or in Gossner's language: the Christ for us and the Christ within us are one. We should keep watch over this unity."[40]

The quest for this inner relationship represents the underlying foundation of the existence of all mission work, first by the individual and then by the church. This is the core of Gossner's apostolic understanding of mission work and the starting point of his action and impact within the mission. Here, Gossner makes no separation between the inner and oversea mission, as introduced by Wichern a generation later. The 'Christ for us' becomes visible both in the needy children and the sick in our own communities and far away, for whom our words and our deeds are important. The individual testimony of the union with Christ at all levels of society and the inseparable connection between the inner and the oversea mission characterise the spiritual legacy of the founder, which calls for reinterpretation in every age.

40 Klaus von Stieglitz, "Gottes Barmherzigkeit hat noch kein Ende" (Klgl. 3, 22). Dank an Vater Gossner, in: Ulrich Schöntube (Hg.): Zwischen Wort und Tat, Beiträge zum 150. Todestag von Johannes Evangelista Gossner, Erlangen 2009, p. 177.

2. Gossner's "Heart of Man" – origin – reception[41]

2.1 Biographical Background

Johannes Evangelista Gossner was born in 1773 in a small town in Hausen in the Baden-Württemberg region of Germany. He grew up in a Catholic family. After studying theology Johannes Gossner came into contact with the Revival-movement. Mainly he sought contact with the Basel Christian Society (Baseler Christenthumsgesellschaft). Founded in 1780, the society wanted to work against the influence of the ideas of the age of Enlightenment. Instead of providing logical explanations of the Bible and its contents, the friends of the Basel Christian Society believed in an education of the heart. This

41 The lecture was held on 28th October 2014. Dr. Wim van Dongen (VU University Amsterdam) and Prof. Sabine Mödersheim (University of Wisconsin – Madison) inspired me for the topic. They researched at the use of heart images in Gossner's "Heart of Man" since 2008. They presented their results at several conferences: 2008: Sabine Mödersheim and Wim van Dongen, "Pure and Impure Hearts: Johannes Gossner's 'The Heart of Man' in Africa". 8th International Conference of the Society for Emblem Studies, Winchester, England, 28th July - 1st August, 2008; 2010: Sabine Mödersheim, "Most Printed Emblems in the World: Johann Gossner's, The Heart of Man'"; Wim van Dongen, "The Global Circulation of an Emblem Book: Johann Gossner's ‚The Heart of Man'". 45th International Congress on Medieval Studies, Kalamazoo Mi, May 13 - 16, 2010. We are waiting for their publication. I am very thankful that Wim van Dongen accompanied his advises in this paper.

is reflected in the title of their magazine: "Collections for lovers of Christian Truth and Godliness" (Sammlungen für Liebhaber christlicher Wahrheit). The magazine has appeared every month since 1786.

In 1811, Gossner was secretary of this society for several months. He even considered at this time to convert to the Lutheran faith. But, he came back after a few months to Munich, where he worked as a catholic chaplain and priest. Inspired by the work in Basel, Gossner wrote a series of smaller spiritual writings during this Munich period. This includes the so-called "Heart booklet", which was published in late summer 1812. The full title is:

> "Heart booklet or the human heart a temple of God or a workshop of Satan in 10 pictures represented symbolically for the promotion and revival of a Christian Mind."[42]

The book is still one of the most successful Christian writings all over the world. What does it contain?

2.2 Content

The book consists of 10 devotions based on engravings. Gossner wanted to show what happens in the soul or in the human heart if Christ moves into it. The heart - it represents the inner man - is disproportionally large in the illustrations, and is surmounted by the head of the believer. Wim van Dongen, a specialist in heart illustrations, named the head with the cheerful wording "Spiritual Selfi".[43]

---

42 "Herzbüchlein oder das Herz des Menschen ein Tempel Gottes oder eine Werkstatt des Satans in 10 Figuren sinnbildlich dargestellt zur Beförderung und Erweckung christlichen Sinnes" The book will be also found with the title: "The Heart of Man. Either a temple of God or the habitation of Satan", Pa 1822.

43 Wim van Dongen (VU University, Amsterdam): "Imagery with a Mission; Gossner and Gschwend on the streets of Lagos, Nigeria". Presentation at 10th International Conference of the Society for Emblem Studies, Kiel, Germany, 28th July - 1st August, 2014.

In the first devotion Gossner describes, what is happening inside a man, who is ruled by sin. According to Catholic tradition the seven deadly sins, symbolized by animals, were depicted in the heart. The 2nd-5th devotions show how the Holy Spirit moves into the heart and how the seven deadly sins are banished from the heart by entering more than seven virtues in their place like faith, hope, charity, humility, generosity, love, chastity, sobriety and patience. Now one might think that the goal has been reached. But now the real danger, the real fight begins. The sixth devotion describes how the faith becomes sleepy. The seventh and eight images depict what happens if the backsliding succeeds. The devil has taken its place in the heart again and the sinner finally dies and goes to the hell. Then the ninth and tenth devotion show what happens for the one, who remains true to his faith. It is as if Gossner wants to say: You can decide, which way you want to go as a Christian at any time. However, you should consider, what the result would be in the end.

2.3 Controversy about the Heart of Man

The "Heart of Man", when it was first published faced a controversial debate. In 1817, five years after the first edition came out, Gossner was summoned regarding this publication before the Dean's Office, which then was responsible for Catholic teaching supervision. Their questions were mainly about the images of the "Heart of Man". Gossner replies:

> "This truth is in the book: rational, scriptural, Christian, catholic; The whole book contains nothing other than the clearest, most useful truths, and I urge every theologian, whether he is Catholic, Lutheran or Calvinist, to try and disprove even one of them.
>
> – But the engravings are absurd and insulting to the zeitgeist (the spirit of the time)!
>
> Well that may be. But the spirit of the time is not the Holy Spirit ... And then:

1. The engravings convey nothing other than the text because the text is only an explanation of the engraving
2. They are only symbols (Sinnbild) of the truth ... No farmer is so stupid that he thinks it is really so in the body; the simple minded in the country know that these engravings are merely useful to symbolise the destruction of a man, who is a slave to his passions ...
3. I have thousands of examples where Symbols have worked effectively and speak to the heart of sensitive people. Even people, who cannot read the text, can understand the symbols, and the pictures are the most instructive part of the book".[44]

The detailed quotation tells at one hand of Gossner's early interdenominational attitude if he urges Catholic, Lutheran and Calvinist theologians to refute in the truths of the book. Here, we meet something, which was later confirmed through anecdote. As Gossner's was asked at a police station which denomination he belonged to, whether Lutheran or Calvinist or Catholic, he replied: "Christian".

On the other hand, Gossner shares the aesthetic assessment, that the images were "absurd and insulting to the zeitgeist (the spirit of the time)." He sees in the pictures more an educational function. Right away, in his first point, he provides an insight into the relationship between word and image. It is not that the images replace the scripture for the layman, as was said by Gregory the Great.[45] But, the texts explain and deepen the understanding of the images. The texts are subordinate to the pictures, so that the images for some readers are the "most instructive" of all. Gossner used here several times the term "sinnbild", which is difficult to translate. Sinnbild pictures symbolize

44 Johann Dettloff Prochnow, Johannes Gossner – Biographie aus Tagebüchern und Briefen, Erster Theil, p. 276, (Transl. U.S.).

45 Gregor der Große: Opera Omnia, Migne Patrologia Latina Vol. 77, Paris 1862, Epistula XIII Ad Serenem Massilliensem Episcopum, 1128 C: "Nam quod legentibus scriptura, hoc idiotis praestat pictura." - Now what for the illiterates the Bible is for the illiterates the image.

something, so the pictures do not tell a biblical story, but express the truth of faith in a symbolic, allegorical or metaphorical way.

At the same time, he admits that the nature of these "Sinnbilder" do not match the zeitgeist (the spirit of the time). These kind of images had apparently gone out of fashion.

2.4 Origin of the images

Over a hundred years earlier, literature with spiritual symbolic images flourished in Europe. "Sinnbild" was at that time a synonymous term for emblems. The emblematic writing was a literary genre, expressing a meaningful truth by linking image and text together. The Milanese lawyer Andreas Alciato 1531 published the first emblem book, "Emblematum liber".[46] It triggered a wide resonance in the 16th and 17th century. An emblem consists generally of three parts, a

Gossner's Heart of Man

Salver, Seelenspiegel 1732

46 Several editions can be found on: http://www.emblems.arts.gla.ac.uk/alciato.

heading (inscriptio), an enigmatic or remarkable image (pictura), and an explanatory text like a poem (subscriptio). By linking the three elements, the reader was able to study moral, philosophical or spiritual issues.

In Gossner's "Heart of Man" we can recognise a late form of this emblem book. The three-part structure is given by the inclusion of the devotions. Without the devotions you cannot interpret the pictures in a proper way. However, text and image relate to each other in Gossner's book. But where did Gossner find these emblems?

a) Salver

Gossner writes in the preface to his little book:

> "This little work was translated from the French and at the earnest request of some pious persons, was published in the year 1732 at Wurtzburg, by the engraver of the University, with the following title: 'Spiritual Mirror of Morality, in which every Christian, who desires his salvation, may view himself, know the state of his soul, and profitably learn to regulate his life according to it.' ... Since 1732, the taste of man has undergone a change – but not the truth – this remains eternally unchangeable … ."[47]

Therefore, Johannes Gossner has invented neither the engravings nor the texts. He has republished and re-edited a book. He refers to an unspecified "Spiritual Mirror of Moral". It is a devotional book from the engraver Johann Salver (1670-1738) from Würzburg. The book was published in 1733. Gossner is not entirely correct in the title. It is not the "Spiritual mirror of Moral" (Geistlicher Sittenspiegel), but the "Spiritual Mirror of the Soul." (Geistlicher Seelenspiegel).[48]

---

47 Johannes Gossner, Heart of Men, Preface. Here is the English edition used: The heart of man: either a temple of God, or a habitation of Satan : represented in ten emblematical figures, calculated to awaken and promote a Christian disposition, ed by Philipp Friedrich Pöschel, Harrisburgh 1851. A full scanned version is available at: https://archive.org/.

48 Johann Salver, Geistlicher Seelenspiegel, in welchem ein jeder seines Heyls begieriger Christenmensch sich ersehen, den Stand seiner Seelen erkennen

Salver, Seelenspiegel, fig. 9 and 12

Gossner did not transfer all of the 12 images from Salver. Gossners elected to use 10 of the illustrations. Furthermore, he revised the texts of the devotions. The omission of 2 images with their devotions is very interesting. Gossner skipped the 9th devotion - it shows the punishing torments of the soul in hell - as well as the 12th the devotion[49], which shows, how the souls of the sinners are fried in the fire and how the pious are fished out of the hellfire.[50]

und seinen Lebenswandel, zu seinem Heyl nützlich danach einrichten kann, Würzburg 1733, Vd 18 12648582001.

49 Peter Daly, The Emblem in Early Modern Europe, Contributions to the Theory of Emblem, Ashgate 2014, p. 218. Daly discovered which illustrations Gossner selected. He states that Gossner did not use plates 5 and 12. The difference with my numbering arises because I used a different edition of the works.

50 Salver, Seelenspiegel, pp. 60-64.

This omission is quite theologically motivated. Obviously Gossner found that a representation of the punishments of hell was dispensable. Maybe he had a similar experience as Martin Luther, who was frightened by these pictures. It can be presumed, that Gossner through these omissions in the new booklet was adapting its contents to suit the actual zeitgeist. The abnegation of the frightening punishing images leads to another reading of the sequence of the images. The presence of the spiritual life is more reflective rather than dwelling on the possible consequences in hell and heaven. The booklet in this abbreviated version asks the reader the question: "Who am I and who reigns in my heart?" - instead of threatening: Look what will happen if you follow a bad way of life. From this background, it is somehow clear why Gossner calls the book "Heart Booklet" or in the English version "Heart of Man". He is concerned with the spiritual self-reflection in the heart. [51]

Miroir de Péchuer

But also Salver did not invent the devotions and engravings.

b) Miroir de Pécheur – Huby, Nobletz

Salver had, as Gossner already mentioned, obviously translated the book from French. Around 1730 in France different editions of an anonymously published mirror of the heart, a so-called "Miroir de Péchuer" [52] were in circulation.

This booklet refers to a 1675 published book entitled "Les images morales et leur explication." It was mainly

51 Gossner's changes need more detailed research by comparing his edition with the source. Here only one obvious example is mentioned.

52 Le Miroir de péchuer, 1739-1754, Bibliothèque nationale de France, département Réserve des livres rares, RES P-YE-2510, http://catalogue.bnf.fr/ark:/12148/cb334885980.

used in Brittany by the Jesuits to re-catholicize this area. Therefore, this book was attributed to two clergy, who worked there, the Jesuit Vincent Huby (1608-1693) and his predecessor the Dominican Michel Le Nobletz (1577-1652). Nobletz tried to bring the people back to the Catholic Church by preaching in Breton (the language of Brittany). He also used the painted charts or educational boards which were produced by Marguerite Alain Lestobec. The pictures were based on the emblematic tradition. These so-called "Taollenou" served him as a specially designed teaching method. The images were initially not printed, but painted on wooden panels. Today only 12-14 "Taollenou" have survived from approximately 70 to 100 pieces in former times. They are treasured at the diocesan town of Quimper.

"Tableaux de Mission" from Quimper (France) from 17th century as archetype for Salver and Gossner.

Nobletz and Lestobec were inspired by a special emblematic tradition. Their inspiration must have come from the Antwerp engraver Anthony Wierix. He was the first one, who represented symbolically the inner emotions of the heart as an image of the human soul. Wierix published in 1595 a cycle with 9 engravings with the title "The sacred heart of the loving Jesus".

Anthony Wierix,
The sacred heart of the loving Jesus

So, if we draw together the sources of Gossner's "Heart of Man". We can combine it in one sentence: Gossner's Book was a re-edition of Salvers Mirror of the Soul, which was itself a translation of an anonymous French devotional book, which was itself attributed to a Jesuit teaching method in Brittany, where missions charts were found, which are inspired by the Emblematic depiction of the heart from the Netherlands. Gossner's "Heart of Man" appears to stem from a Jesuit tradition, which was used by the Counter-Reformation. It is remarkable that Gossner's Book is still in use today, especially in Protestant missionary work with an incredible distribution. Possibly Gossner's reformulated devotions and his strategy of omitting the representations of punishments of the hell were the key to the success of the booklet.

2.5 Reception

a) Adaptation to the Cultural Background

The reception of the "Heart of Man" is very difficult to understand. The first English translation appears in 1822 in Pennsylvania. German immigrant communities had brought the booklet to America. In the period just after this, a vast number of German and English editions of the booklet appeared in America.

Various editions of the book were used to great effect by the Mission in 19th and 20th century. In this regard, numerous examples can be found in the library of the Gossner Mission. The images were modified and adapted to the cultural realities. This can be seen not only on the surmounted human head. For example, even the animals that symbolized the "Deadly Sins" were culturally adjusted depending on the context. An insight might be seen in the Tamil edition of 1932:

Gossner's Heart of Man,
Tamil Edition, 1874

Gossner's Heart of Man,
German edition, 1815

We see a change of the animals in this process of inculturation: A proud lion replaces the peacock, a rat replaces the turtle, an avaricious elephant/ dung beetle replaces the European toad, a dog replaces the angry leopard, and a vulture replaces the envious snake. However, the various uses of the tradition of illustration in the different cultural contexts needs to be more accurately researched.

A special treasure of Gossner Mission library is a hand-coloured Urdu edition in Latin script. Again we notice cultural adaptations by recognising the influence of the Arabian tradition of book painting.

Heart of Men, Urdu edition from 1890,
Library of Gossner Mission

b) Gschwend

The history of "Heart of Man" took a new turn particularly in the 20th and 21st centuries. This is linked with the story of J. R. Gschwend. The Swiss soldier J. R. Gschwend was captured by the

Germans in the First World War and under suspicion of espionage was sentenced to death. In his prison cell, he experienced a conversion to God and he decided to serve God in an extraordinary way. When the Germans released him without any explanation, he started studying to become a pastor. In 1921, he travelled to Africa and founded in 1935 a still existing mission-publishing house, the All Nations Gospel Publishers. The bestseller from the beginning was the "Heart of Man" in various translations. By 1929, Gschwend had rewritten the texts of the devotion, but without mentioning his source as Johannes Gossner. Since then, the book has been published in 450 languages. Annually there were thirty new translations added. International emblematic specialist, who observing the scene, estimate the number of copies is easily in Millions.[53]

Similar to the Taollenou in Brittany, the images of Gschwend are also used as plates for Evangelisation. In the Internet you will find today also several films on the use of the plates "Heart of Man".

The history of Heart of Men is not finished yet. Some questions remain unclear. Thus, the various traditional types of illustration will need to be described in more detail, looking at the attempts made at enculturation. Furthermore, the changes in the text need to be researched, both those undertaken by Gossner and by Gschwend. The combination of image and text is the reason for the success of the book. Even till today, it is probably, after the Bible, one of the world's most popular books of Christian literature.

53 Wim van Dongen, at the 10th conference of the International Society of Emblem Studies in Kiel 2014, presented various editions of Gschwend for several countries.

3. "... and covered me with kisses..." – Johann Hinrich Wichern (1808-1881) visiting Johannes Evangelista Gossner in Berlin[54]

It was a mild summer evening, and the young man's heart was beating fast, when he opened the garden door of the Elisabeth Hospital in Berlin, Potsdamer Strasse. Flowers were blooming in front of the summer-house. It was silent. The young man, who was approaching the house was the 33 year old Johann Hinrich Wichern. When Wichern lived in Berlin, he used to relate all that happened to him there, to his wife Amanda who was back in Hamburg. This was also the case after he visited Gossner. He met Gossner on July 1st, 1841. Wichern writes:

> "In the evening I went to see Gossner. I entered his house with great joy. His Missionary activities have always appealed to me, more than anything else. He lives in a pleasant summer-house, with many flowers blooming in front of it. This is where we sat down."[55]

54 Lecture held on 3rd March 2008 during a Seminar on the occasion of 150th anniversary of father Gossner's day of death.

55 Quoted from: D. Johann Hinrich Wichern: Gesammelte Schriften D. Johann Hinrich Wicherns. Briefe und Tagebuchblätter D. Johann Hinrich Wicherns, I. Band 1826-1848, Hamburg 1901, p. 266. Unfortunatly we have no complete

The year 2008 was a jubilee year of Wichern and Gossner. It was the 200th anniversary of the birth of Johann Hinrich Wichern, "father" of the "Innere Mission" (i.e. the Church social service to the needy in the Church's home country or home context, otherwise called "Diakonie" = Diaconate), and it was the 150th anniversary of the death of Johannes Evangelista Gossner. Wichern has come to be recognised as very important for the development of the Evangelical Church and the Christian Diaconate in Germany. His historical importance has produced an extensive body of literature, none of which has dealt, it is true, with his links to Gossner, although both met quite often in Berlin. This present essay tries to close this gap by looking at the historical context and at the approaches of the two theologians.

3.1 The two men and their time

The question of social injustice needed to be urgently addressed in Germany. In the beginning of the 19th century "Leibeigenschaft" (rural serfdom) had been abolished through the reforms of the Prussian minister Heinrich Carl Friedrich vom und zum Stein (1757-1831). Many men and women moved away from countryside and tried to settle in the cities, which at the same time were in the grip of industrialisation. Factories grew up. Hand-made products could not compete with mass production. People lived in "Mietskasernen" (tenement houses) in apartments much too small for their extended families. In most cases, just one family member was able to earn money. Hence, greater parts of the population lived in poverty. Both Wichern and Gossner reacted to this social situation in similar ways.

---

edition of all letters of Wichern. The edition I use is from Wichern's son. But, the letters were not correctly edited in some cases. The problem of the editing of Wichern's letters: Volker Herrmann: Innere Mission und Diakonie bei Johann Hinrich Wichern, in: Volker Herrmann/ Jürgen Gohde/ Heinz Schmidt (Hg.): Johann Hinrich Wichern – Erbe und Auftrag. Stand und Perspektiven der Forschung, Heidelberg 2007, p. 133.

When they met in Gossner's summer-house in 1841, Wichern could already look back on a remarkable success. At the age of only 25 years, having finished his university theological studies, he founded a children's home, "Rettungsanstalt", a rescue institute, the so-called "Rauhes Haus", in his home city Hamburg, Germany. He did this without any state or community subsidy. The house became an establishment for the care of children who were described as "difficult or neglected".[56] Here, such children could grow up in small family-like groups.

Also Gossner's manifold activities had some years earlier resulted in the foundation of an institute in Berlin. The beginning was very modest.[57] An acquaintance of Gossner's, a servant from Russia, fell ill. Gossner tried to help him and asked some friends to assist. This was the starting point for a "Maenner-Krankenverein" (men's health association), a visiting service for the care of the sick. A special call for donations later helped to create a parallel women's health service. Friedrike Graefin von Reeden (1774-1854) became so active in support of the health association that finally an apartment had to be rented in Hirschelstrasse, Berlin, where sick people could be admitted for stationary medical care. Soon after, a piece of land had to be bought outside the inner city. The King of Prussia and several Berlin citizens helped to finance the creation of the Elisabeth Hospital in 1836 on this piece of land. In Gossner's understanding, salvation and healing belonged together.

3.2 The Meeting

One could think, that at their first meeting in 1841 the two men would have discussed the conceptions of Evangelical diaconate. But, the meeting turned out quite differently. Wichern reports:

> "A few minutes later we were having a lively debate. My question had been: How do you prepare your messengers to

56 He calls his house: "Institution for difficult to educate and neglected children".

57 Hermann Dalton, Johannes Gossner, p. 359f.

the heathens for their Missionary service? - He, unwillingly: Why do you ask so? The reason for his displeasure was that he believed me to be one of the people, who were criticizing the practices in his Missionary service. He then spoke about the great deal of annoyance the critics were causing him. This was unknown to me, but he had thought, I knew about it. Then he spoke with great displeasure about the kind of preparatory training for missionaries that was practised in the Mission centres. To discuss this issue with Gossner was important to me because he was sending out people to America too, and he knew that I was occupied with the same kind of tasks. Finally, he declared his full agreement with what he had heard from me on this subject, and he obviously liked my report."[58]

Indeed Gossner had distanced himself from the normal practice of the Mission societies. Initially in 1831 he had become member of the Committee of the Berlin Mission society, but five years later he renounced any cooperation with them. This dispute echoed in his dialogue with Wichern. In Gossner's opinion, missionaries who were not theologians, they should be equipped with a faithful heart and good Bible knowledge. As missionaries in far away countries they should, like St. Paul the apostle, earn their living through working with their hands. This was contrary to the principles of the Berlin Mission society, which insisted on sending out only fully trained, graduated theologians.

This conflict had developed earlier. Already in 1833, Gossner was honoured to preach during a service for the benefaction of missionaries in the Dreifaltigkeitskirche (Trinity Church) from the pulpit of the famous Prof. Friederich Schleiermacher (1768-1834).[59] In his sermon, he had declared the spreading of the Gospel to be a

58 D. Johann Hinrich Wichern, Briefe und Tagebuchblätter, p. 270.

59 For the biographical background see the article "Johannes Evangelista Gossner" in this book.

prime task for every Christian, not only for the professionally trained one. In his words:

> "I therefore affirm: evangelical missions, or the preaching of the Gospel to all nations and at all times, and thus the sending forth of evangelical preachers to all nations and at all times, for the planting and dissemination of Christianity, for the happiness of the nations, of our fellow man and our brothers, who have also been redeeming, is the task which is the most indispensable and based in the nature of Christianity, and at the same time, the most blessed and most gratifying business, the holiest and most important duty, which every Christian, and the entire Church, should make their own."[60]

In this quotation, we find summarized the essential marks of the idea of Mission in the thinking of our Mission father Gossner. We find first the already mentioned feature that the spreading of Christianity should not be bound to the profession of the theologian or pastor. Every Christian is a missionary. On the other hand, we find here already Gossner's integrating concept of Mission: The spreading of Christianity is a "blessing for all people", and they are for "our fellow-men." So, mission is not only directed to people far away but also to those nearby. External and internal cannot be separated. Gossner's and Wichern's positions are near to each other in the first point, but fundamentally different in the second. This will be outlined in the following paragraphs.

a) Everyone is a missionary

Wichern sees the social distress as an expression for lack of faith among the people. In his "Denkschrift" (memorandum) with which the work of the Inner Mission in Germany was founded, he explains that from the beginning of Christianity the lasting issue has been and still is the spreading and accomplishing of God's Kingdom in

60 This quote is cited in: Hans Lokies, Johannes Gossner, p. 71.

all areas of life, namely the state and community, art and science, and social life. The whole nation should grow into a nation of active Christians, with constitutions and orders according to the Kingdom of God. But in the areas of family, property and labour, "the spirit of faithlessness– and consequently moral decadence – is increasing".[61] In the beginning of Christianity, Love was conceivable only inside the closed circle of disciples, as is demonstrated in the "valedictory addresses" in St. John's Gospel (John 13-17). But, Wichern thinks this love will only come to its universal destination when all people still standing outside the Christian community will be overcome by the power of love.[62.] With this overflowing love they will keep the Saviour in their midst, because in their living together and loving each other "His life and His love will be manifest".[63]

> With this overflowing love "the community of the Lord ...will become a blessed community of priests, a kingly people of God in which everyone, having received the Lord's witness, will himself bear witness to His life, proclaiming out of an inner necessity the goodness of Him, who has called him from the darkness into His marvellous light. The priesthood of all believers is at the same time their consecration into the service of Mission, also the Inner Mission."[64]

With this concept Wichern seems to come very near towards Gossner's notion of the Mission service to be every Christian's obligation. Wichern's assumption is that Christ is present in the

61 Johann Hinrich Wichern, Denkschrift, in: Sämtliche Werke, Bd. I, Hamburg 1962, p. 160.

62 Johann Hinrich Wichern, Sämtliche Werke I, p. 63: Im engsten Kreis der Liebe "liegt die Möglichkeit und Bestimmung .... einst der allumfassende zu werden, nach dem alle die, welche zunächst außerhalb des Kreises stehen, Nächste oder Feinde, von der ihm innewohnenden Liebensmacht werden überwunden sein.

63 Ibid., p. 64.

64 Johann Hinrich Wichern, Zwölf Thesen, in: Sämtliche Werke III/1, p. 206, (Transl. U.S.).

overflowing love. Gossner, too, develops his notion of Mission from a Christological background, but with a more individualistic personal impetus. His concern is with the personal association with Christ in ones heart. He shows this for instance in his "Herzbüchlein" (Heart of Man), edited some years before. Following this thought, all negative actions of the heart such as envy, greed, etc., will leave a person as soon as Christ comes, with his redeeming love, into their heart. What happens in the heart is a substantial change. Hence, personal communion with Christ is the aim of missionary activity, of both inner and oversea Missions.[65] Therefore, a missionary does not need to have studied, but needs to have the communion with Christ in his heart. Therefore, a missionary is anyone, who has got the "Herzensbildung" (education of the heart) through Christ. Gossner is more concerned with the opening of the individual heart for Christ, whereas Wichern sees in the foreground the human social community thoroughly reformed by the Love of Christ. But both agree that Mission is every Christian's vocation.

b) Inner Mission – Oversea Mission

Both Gossner and Wichern were theologians of the Revival movement, which can be seen in the christological core of their concepts of Mission, although each placed their own emphasis on different aspects of this concept. The greatest difference between them both was the question of which direction the Mission should take.

In 1848, representatives of all regional Evangelical churches in Germany met in the city of Wittenberg. They discussed what the response of the Church should be to the revolution of 1848. An Evangelical union of Churches was founded. Wichern took part in this congress. When the meeting came to the subject of the question of social injustice, Wichern rose to speak. As he later reported to his wife, he "delivered a spontaneous speech of five quarters of an hour, produced on the spot".[66] His thesis was: Social need and

65 Walter Holsten, Johann Evangelista Gossner, p. 28.

66 D. Johann Hinrich Wichern: Briefe und Tagebuchblätter, p. 453.

demoralisation both being caused by lack of faith, so the people had to be guided "back to the divine Word and Spirit".[67] Upon this, the entire assembly declared the matter of Inner Mission to be a particular and special task of the Church. From then on till today the Diaconate remains a major field of work for the Church, often with the congregation and local church as counterparts. Gossner, too, saw the necessity to witness Christian faith in his own home country. But for him – in my judgement this was where he was forward-looking – there is merely one indivisible Mission of God, in which men and women can participate as His witnesses. Oversea Mission abroad, which is the sending out of missionaries to other countries or regions, and Inner Mission, which is the witness of faith in a person's own environment through word and deed, belong together as do two twin sisters. This finds it's symbolic expression in the fact, that in the same year 1836 the Elisabeth hospital was founded and six missionaries were accepted by Gossner and their education started by him in preparation for their service abroad. Another aspect of Gossner' foresight, which should not be ignored, was to combine both the oversea and inner Mission with each other with the idea of integrating them. This was expressed in a cheerful emblem. Gossner called his first information paper "The bee on the Mission field". He means that this insect, having collected honey in far-away fields, will bring honey from there – so to speak for the revival of Christians at home![68] This image expresses the opportunities that area created where there is a common understanding of combining both fields. Both can enrich each other.

Despite the differences between them, all his life Wichern was filled with a deep respect for Gossner.[69] When they first met, their differences concerning the question of Mission were not obvious.

67 Johann Hinrich Wichern, Denkschrift, in Sämtliche Werke Bd. I, p. 163f.

68 The emblem is explained at the beginning of the paper "The Jubilee Centenary of Edinburgh 1910-2010 and its heritage today" in this book.

69 This became obvious in Wicherns obituary. Sometimes Wichern refers to Gossners work. For instance, in the 16th letter to the Brothers of his "Rauhen Haus" he describes Gossner as an old honourable father. Wichern: Sämtliche Werke VIII, p. 130.

At the time Wichern himself was planning to send out missionaries, as he revealed in his letter. Both of them felt they were theologians of the Revivalist Movement and very much bound to each other in their efforts to lead people to Christ. That is why it came to the following scene of deeply-felt friendship in which Wichern, certainly not without pride, could report to his wife:

> "Soon we were called in to tea. Afterwards I left. But he tried to be alone with me, hugged me and covered me with kisses ... and asked me to visit him again."[70]

70 D. Johann Hinrich Wichern: Briefe und Tagebuchblätter, p. 270.

Section 2

Lutheran Heritage

1. Luther and the Arts[71]

It is very much inspired to think about our common Lutheran heritage regarding art and liturgy because we start recently a musical exchange. In Germany, it is occasionally questioned whether we as followers of father Gossner in the missio Dei should deepen in our partnership the musical cooperation. Aren't there more important things to do in the work of the church, for instance concerning the social miseries? Certainly one can point to the mission father himself, of whom it has been said that he taught his congregation a song, which he had spontaneously composed.

But, I want to look even further back, namely to the Reformation and our common heritage. I believe that by looking at how art was dealt with within the Lutheran Reformation principles, we can learn how we can theologically evaluate the music and what recommendations can be made for a culturally correct proclamation of the Gospel.

The Wittenberg Reformation was art-promoting and art appreciating in every respect. In this regard, it did not differ so strongly from the Catholic Church; it did however differ from the later art-puritanical reform movement. It is only in the function of the art, that one sees a difference to the Catholic tradition. If, in the late medieval tradition, art served the Catholic Church as their representation of holiness, then in contrast art in the protestant

71 Lecture was held on 31st October, 2007.

tradition was used to communicate the Gospel. This spiritual historical change in the theological handling of art is particularly highlighted in the "painting controversy". We will look at this first and then I would like us to consider Luther's attitude to the use of music. With these two exemplary fields of art, the principles will be revealed, which will help us in the present evaluation of the relationship between music and mission.

1.1 Luther and Paintings

If now we want to concentrate on the picture controversy, then we must begin in the year 1522 in the city of Wittenberg, where the Reformation movement started. Luther was kept in the Wartburg Castle in the winter of 1521/22, since he was considered an outlaw - vogelfrei. While Luther was there, the Wittenberg city council authorized the removal of imagery from churches with a special act that specified: "Also the pictures and altars in the churches should be removed."[72] Since the implementation of this new order was not immediate, Andreas Bodenstein of Carlstadt had time to write an article, and this had immediate consequences. It was called "On the Dismissal of Pictures and that there should be no Christian beggars" which appeared in Wittenberg 1522 in two editions.[73] This circulated relatively quickly. As a result there was an iconoclasm; the castle church's side altar was violently ransacked by the masses. This

72 Hans Lietzmann (Hg.), Die Wittenberger Ordnung von 1522, Kleine Texte Nr. 21, Berlin 1931, p. 5. Nr. 13. But this Act – and that is not remarked in reformation history – was not printed in Wittenberg itself, but in Speyer and Augsburg. Siegfried Bräuer: Umgestaltung und Übergänge. Beobachtungen zu den Anfängen des reformatorischen Gottesdienstes, in: Revue d' Histoire et de Philosophie Religieuses, 85 (2005) p. 65. It might be questioned, if this act has really this wide effect in Wittenberg.

73 Andreas Bodenstein von Karlstadt, Von der abthuung der bylder/ vnnd das keyn Betler under den Christen seyn soll, Wittenberg 1522, herausgegeben von Hans Lietzmann, Kleine Texte für theologische und philosophische Vorlesungen und Übungen, Nr. 74, Bonn 1911. Ernst Ullmann, Die Wittenberger Unruhen, Andreas Bodenstein von Karlstadt und die Bilderstürme in Deutschland, in: L'Art et les révolutions, Actes du XXVIIe congrès international d'histoire de l'Art, Bd. 4, 1992, p. 117-126.

action was outrageous, especially when taking into consideration the piousness of the people in the middle-ages. This is because altars and church relics were worshiped and it was believed that the Saints were actually present in them. Also, Luther's Elector-Prince, Friedrich the Wise, had the largest relic collection of his time. So, what were the arguments that could mobilize the masses in such a manner as to cause them to revolt against the pictures?

Andreas Bodenstein of Carlstadt, who came to be known simply as Carlstadt, was Luther's colleague at the University of Wittenberg. The basis of his arguments was biblical in nature - specifically concerning the First Commandment.

> "See how God forbids all pictures / because the people are gullible and tend towards worshipping them. ... Also when one would say, 'Yes I don't pray to the pictures or idolize them as pictures, but rather because of the holiness that they represent.' God answers to that with short simple words."[74]

Because it is written: You shall not make for yourself an idol. As it is clear to see in this quote, Carlstadt had a very specific anthropological view based on the absolute validity of the first Commandment. It negated any differentiation in the relationship between humans and the pictures. It was not possible for them to look at pictures as a reminder,[75] or as a reference, without them being worshiped at the same time in their hearts. Carlstadt felt: Those who look upon a picture, worship it.[76] He recommended therefore the removal of pictures, because they tempt humans to Idol-worship.

74 Andreas Bodenstein von Karlstadt: Von der abthuung der bylder (About the Rejection of images), p. 7, 74-31 (Transl. U.S.).

75 Ibid., p. 16, 12-19: "If somebody says the pictures remind us to the passion of our Lord ... then answer: God forbid images. Also Christ says that God is a Spirit. All, who truly pray to God, they pray through the Spirit. John 4. All who pray to God through pictures they pray in lie, in illusoriness and in external annunciation they remember God. But the heart is pious from God and they make him to an idol in their heart ... " (Transl. U.S.).

76 Margarete Stirm, Bilderfrage in der Reformation, Gütersloh 1977, p. 38.

Humans were therefore incapable of giving the honour solely to God.

When Luther heard of the tumultuous events in Wittenberg, he emerged out of his hiding place in Wartburg Castle. The Elector-Prince, Friedrich the Wise, had warned him in a letter, he could not protect Luther any more if he left the Wartburg Castle. Luther answered him, if he did not go now, he would not be able to protect the Elector any longer. The Reformer arrived in the first week of Lent and held his famous Invocavit sermons.

Which position did he adopt to end the violence and then did he have to plead for the return of the artwork? At first, he very clearly showed restraint in his sermon regarding the pictures:

> "Now we come to the pictures: If we look at it this way, they aren't necessary, but free, we can take them or leave them… however it would be better if we didn't have them. I don't like them either… and I wish they would be abolished in the whole world because of the abuse which is made of them, which one cannot deny."[77]

One could assume now that Luther would take a similar stance as Carlstadt did in his Lent Sermons – that pictures can entice humans to worship falsely. However, for Luther, the subsequent logical conclusion was not that the pictures must be removed. Then there is a difference between the object itself and the person who look at the object. It is the person, who uses works of art to lift himself up. Therefore it is the person and not the pictures that should be held responsible if he abuses them to his own detriment. Luther brings jovial examples of what would follow from such a categorical misunderstanding within other areas of human existence.

> "Furthermore, the woman and wine bring some people misfortune and turn them into fools, therefore does this mean that we want to kill all women and pour away all the

77 Martin Luther Werke, Kritische Gesamtausgabe, Weimar (WA) 10,3, p. 26, 4-6 and p. 31,1-3 (Transl. U.S.).

> wine. Ah, if we want to get rid of our worst enemy, the one who is most damaging to us, then we need to kill ourselves, for we have no greater enemy than our own hearts."[78]

Carlstadt, by removing the pictures, proves the opposite of what he is preaching. By demanding the removal of the artwork he substantiates the power that proceeds from them. Since humans can be tempted by the mere presence of pictures, in Carlstadt's mind they should be removed. For Luther, this power of the pictures is non-existent.

In his opinion, through the "Abolishing" of the pictures, the danger and the power of what are essentially neutral objects, is particularly emphasised. The removal of them testifies to the power that the pictures have on the faithful, and therefore the removal of the pictures does not fulfil the first commandment but actually violates it. Thus, Luther accuses Carlstadt: "... you will make their case much stronger using these methods (the removal)".[79]

Luther emphasizes however that in order to change the hearts of the faithful one must do so through vigorous preaching of the Gospel so that the worship of the pictures and the associated abuse ends.

If one regards Luther's attitude in this controversy, then it seems the art in the pictures has in fact hardly anything positive to offer. Pictures are, as Luther said, free. That is, they have hardly any meaning for humans freed by the Gospel. This was the year 1522.

A few years later, in 1525, it appears there is a change in his detached attitude toward pictures. In his treatise "Wider die himmlischen Propheten" (Against the Heavenly Prophets)[80] he argues again with the views of Carlstadt and his followers.

According to Luther in regards to the pre-Reformation art, one should not indiscriminately destroy everything. One could allow the

78 WA 10,3, p. 33, 12-34, 2 (Transl. U.S.).

79 WA 10,3, p. 29,5-9 (Transl. U.S.).

80 English translation by: Bernhard Erling, in: Luther Works Vol. 40, Philadelphia 1958.

people "a crucifix, or an icon … to gaze at, to testify, to remind, to symbolize", since Jesus himself tolerated sinful pictures, such as the portrait of the Caesar.[81] After all, Luther saw himself the iconoclasts reading in his German Bible.[82] Here is where the educational tradition of the Lutheran use of pictures begins. And it culminates in 1529, the year in which Luther's two Catechisms appeared. Luther published for the first time a Biblical picture book, the so-called Passional. It was an appendix to a prayer booklet, which appeared first in 1521. The booklet with the Passional was a best seller, because in the period of 1529-1600 at least 55 editions were published.[83] It is in the preface to the Passional that the educational use of pictures is explicitly unfolded as being positive. Let us hear a longer quotation from the preface:

> "I thought it was good thing to add the Passional booklet to the prayer book, especially because of the children and simple people, who would be better inspired to retain the godly stories through pictures and parables, than through the word or lessons alone. As Saint Mark testified, that for the sake of the simple people Christ also preached in Parables… For it is true one cannot represent or illustrate the works of God enough for the common man. When one immediately sings, says, rings out, preaches, writes, reads, draws and sketches them, even then is Satan always there all too strong and brave, in order to hinder and suppress one with his angels and subordinates, so that such intensions and endeavours are not in and of themselves enough, but

81 WA 18, p. 80, 6-14. (Transl. U.S.).

82 WA 18, pp. 82, 21-83, 5. So we request them in a friendly way that they would paint those pictures at the walls for memory and better understanding. … It is better they paint, how God creates the world, how Noah constructed the Ark … According to God's will I would request all the rich people that they paint the whole biblical story inside and outside the houses for everybody's eyes. That would be a Christian work." (Transl. U.S.)

83 Peter van der Coelen, Bilder aus der Schrift, Studien zur alttestamentlichen Druckgraphik des 16. und 17. Jahrhunderts, Bern 2002, p. 49.

also necessary and most urgent .... I have however added a few stories and Psalms from the Bible, so that both would help one to be more secure and they would be more firmly retained."[84]

One can glean from Luther's preface several recommendations. They concern a) the addressees, b) the purpose of the intercession, and c) the methodology of the instruction.

A) Addressee: First, the pictures are meant for indoctrination. Luther has in mind "children", "simple people" and the "common man". That was in its time a social rank, or caste. Craftsmen with a simple education belonged likewise to it as well as apprentices. One must know that in those days at the most only half of the population was literate in the cities.[85] But, Luther seems to follow the medieval tradition of Gregory the Great, who thought that pictures are the books of the laymen.[86]

B) The Purpose: The laypeople should be able to remember the Biblical stories. Therefore, they cannot be preached, painted and sung enough. Here, in my opinion, Luther undertakes a restriction according to the medieval tradition, which can be perceived only at second glance. It was in the middle-ages that the idea developed in the scholastic textbooks, in the tradition of Gregory, that pictures are books of the laymen. For Bonaventura for example, whom Luther had studied, pictures are there for the layman so 1) they will be introduced into the secrets of the faith, 2) that their dispositions and their emotions will be moved and 3) their memory

84 WA 10,2, pp. 458, 16-21.30 - 459, 2.

85 Rolf Engelsing, Analphabetentum und Lektüre, Zur Sozialgeschichte des Lesens in Deutschland zwischen feudaler und industrieller Gesellschaft, Stuttgart 1973.

86 Gregor der Große, Opera Omnia, Migne Patrologia Latina Vol. 77, Paris 1862, Epistula XIII Ad Serenem Massilliensem Episcopum, 1128 C: "Nam quod legentibus scriptura, hoc idiotis praestat pictura ... ." Now what for the illterates the Bible is for the illiterates the image.

will be challenged.[87] With this background we see that Luther limits the effect of the picture for the laymen only to the last point, the memory. That comes from his fundamental position of neutrality, which he had expounded upon in the Invocavit sermons. Here, we are looking at exactly the same thing. Pictures do not have power over the beholder. Therefore, they cannot cause an emotion or instruct in secrets of the faith, but how can pictures help develop memory?

C) Methodology: We see also here a clear divergence from Gregory's tradition, to regard pictures as layman's books. Luther says, that biblical images cannot be presented with "too many or too often". This basically means pictures are a way of remembering, but nothing more. They replace neither the reading of the Scripture nor the sermons nor the Hymns. Therefore sermons, writing, painting and reading are equal to each other. Therefore - as the methodology of remembering Biblical stories – pictures should be used in conjunction with the written word. Thus, Luther in the preface to the Passional, stated that he had arranged both together in his booklet as examples of this.

In practical analysis this means Luther's attitude towards pictures, was that he preferred Biblical representations. He rejected pictures of

87 Johannes Bonaventura, Commentaria in quattuor Libros sententiarum Magisteri Petri Lombardi, Tert. Lib. Dist. IX, Art. I, qu. II. Opera Omnia, Quaracchhi Rom 1892-1902, p. 203: "Propter simplicium ruditatem inventae sunt (scil. picturae), ut simplices, qui non possunt scripturas legere, in huiusmodi sculpturis et picturis tanquam in scripturis apertuis possint sacramenta nostrae fidei legere. – Propter affectus tarditatem similiter introductae sunt … Plus enim excitatur affectus noster per ea quae videt, quam per ea quae audit. … Propter memoriae labilitatem, quia ea quae audiuntur solum, facilius traduntur oblivioni, quam ea quae videntur. Frequenter enim verificatur in multis illud quod consuevit dici: verbum intrat per unam aurem et exit per aliam."

the medieval tradition like that of the "Church-Ship"[88], as well as various depictions of Mary, which damaged the dignity of Christ.[89]

Let us summarize Luther's attitude towards pictures and consequently try to develop some principles in dealing with art, which we can compare with his attitude to music. First, pictures do not have any characteristic, with which they exercise power over humans. If humans are moved in their hearts by a picture, then it is an impulse of the recipient and has nothing to do with picture and its aura. This was the crucial difference between Carlstadt and Luther. Furthermore, pictures have a function to repeat Biblical stories and engrain their message. But therein they do not have primacy in relation to other ways of promulgation. Singing, painting, preaching and reading are equally important to each other. To that extent the pictures are also not a replacement for the sermon or the scripture reading. Luther is rather reserved, in relation to the high esteem in which pictures were held in medieval theology. He minimalized the effect of picture according to the medieval tradition. He considers the picture as an object. Beyond that, there are pictures that give people a wrong view of God, a conception, which does not have anything to do with the love of God and freedom of the Doctrine of Justification through faith.

1.2 Luther and Music

Already in childhood music was a part of Luther's life. He attended a Latin school in Mansfeld. Part of the tasks of the students was to assist

88 WA 38, p. 104,16-34. The Church Ship was a special type of picture in medieval age representing the church. Inside the ship were to be seen the clergy people and outside in the water the congregation seeking rescue from that ship of salvation. It expresses that the church gives through their sacraments the salvation. Luther criticises that not the church but the faith brings God's grace to the people.

89 WA 47, p. 276, 21-27: "It is idolatry to send the people under the mantle of Mary like some of the preachers and monks did. They paint mother Mary, that Christ holds in his hand three arrows, one was pest, the other war, the third price increase to punish the people; here mother Mary opens their mantle to protect the people from punishment." (Transl. U.S.).

in the worship by singing in the Boys choir. His musical education was continued with his study in Erfurt. Luther studied at first law. As part of this basic education was the study of the seven liberal arts: grammar, rhetoric, logic (Trivium) geometry, arithmetic, music, and astronomy (Quadrivium). A close fellow student from his time there recalled in 1520, half a generation later, in particular Luther's musical abilities. He writes: "Eras in nostro quondam contubernio musicus et philosophicus eruditis" - you were among us study comrades the musician and experienced philosopher.[90] Luther's instrument was the lute. His opponents even mocked him about it. Johannes Cochlaeus, a humanist, who challenged Luther to a theological duel at the Diet of Worms (the Assembley of German Principals), was amused by it in his writing "De actis et scripsis Lutheri". Luther is an "Orpheus in monks robe and tonsure".[91] The writings of Cochlaeus from the 16th Century, by the way, shaped the Catholic evaluation of Luther into the 20th Century.[92] Luther's house in Wittenberg held a very special place for the practise of the musical arts. There are numerous suggestions and remarks made by his pupils, where it is mentioned that after dinner one made music.[93] Luther writes with humour to the composer Matthias Weller from Freiberg, who had sent him a choral arrangement, a Canticum, on 18 January 1535:

> "We sing as well as we can, at the table, and then pass it on. If we make some sod (sic, means mistake) of it, then it is certainly not your fault, but our talent, which is still very little... ."[94]

---

90 Ernst Ludwig Enders, Luthers Briefwechsel, Erlangen 1884, Vol. 2, p. 183, 391.

91 Historia J. Cochlaei de actis et scripsis M. Lutheri, Köln 1568, p. 55.

92 Adolf Herte, Die Lutherbiographie des Johannes Cochläus. Eine quellenkritische Untersuchung, Diss. Münster 1915.

93 Christian Gotthold Neudecker, Die handschriftliche Geschichte Ratzebergers über Luther und seine Zeit, Jena 1850, p. 59.

94 Martin Leberecht de Wette, Luthers Briefe von seinem Aufenthalt auf der Coburger Veste während des Reichstags zu Augsburg, bis zur Schließung der Wittenberger Konkordie, Vol. 4, Berlin 1824, p. 586 (Transl. U.S.).

The practice of music can thus be testified to quite cheerfully. Above all there are many songs, which Luther wrote himself and many are also known here in Ranchi. These are also a witness to Luther's practical knowledge of music.

Now, how did Luther evaluate music as a theologian? In order to answer this question, we will turn to three classical sources, a letter to a Bavarian composer, a preface to a choral piece and the Hymnbook Preamble.

a) The Letter

Ludwig Senfl (1486-1543) was court musician for the Bavarian king Wilhelm IV (1493-1550). Luther wrote to him in 1535, because he apparently wanted a choral arrangement for his house musicians. It dealt with a song, where the melody was one that he had enjoyed since his youth. Before stating his request in the letter, he makes the following observations about music. He praises the catholic Prince Senfls, since he preserves and esteems music.

> "There is no doubt that many seeds of good virtue are in those souls who commit themselves to music. Those who aren't affected by it have similarities to tree trunks and stones. ... And I quite believe and am not ashamed to claim that after theology no art can equal that of music ("post theologiam esse nullam artem, quae musicam aequari"), because next to theology only it allows what theology creates elsewhere, namely, tranquillity and peace of the soul. Thus it is clearly proven that the devil flees as instigator of sad concerns and restless confusion from the voice of music almost in the same way as from the word of theology."[95]

Thus, music stands before all arts and it is alike to theology in the fact that it drives out the devil of sadness. What theology is able to do through the word of Grace, music is able to do through

95 Martin Luther, Briefe, Eine Auswahl, herausgegeben von Günter Wartenberg, Leipzig 1983, p. 182 (Transl. U.S).

harmony. Luther therefore justifies the proximity between theology and music biblically. Already with the prophets it could be seen that they spoke the truth in Psalms and song and they did not need "geometry, arithmetic and astronomy" (Quadrivium). Let us dare to make a comparative glance at the picture. Obviously with the use of pictures one could not revert to such a biblical reflection. On the contrary, there was a Biblical Iconoclasm here. But I'm jumping ahead. Let us look at a second locus classicus, the preface to the choir hymnbook.

b) Simphoniae iucundae

It was in the year 1538, that the Wittenberg printer George Rhaw (1488-1548) published a collection of choral pieces. He was particularly gifted in his field, because prior to his work as a printer he had been the Choirmaster of the St. Thomas Choir in Leipzig, a position in which J. S. Bach would later bring about the blossoming of protestant Church music. Luther's Latin preface to this work was translated in various ways and passed on. It is therefore also to be found in Luther's work under the title "Tribute to music". First, Luther states that music is a gift of God's creation. Music meets us everywhere. There is nothing in nature, which is without sound and rhythm. But nothing, according to Luther, is comparable to the human voice. Humankind, in comparison to nature, is "given a singing voice allied with speech, so that he knows that he must praise God with word and music, specifically through the mixed language of a ringing sermon and a lovely melody."[96] Also here Luther points to the biblical scriptures. The prophets would have adhered to this by using the Psalms. A further parallel to the letter that he had written to Senfl three years earlier concerns the psychological effects of music. He writes however without comparing the music to the word of God:

96 Martin Luther Taschenausgabe in fünf Bänden, Vol. 2, p. 182.

> "Then what is more effective than music to encourage the sad, to frighten the merry, to encourage those in despair, to humble the proud, to pacify the impassioned."

Music affects the human spirit thus directly. Who does not recognize that is, according to Luther, not only untalented, but he hears only the music of pigs and bad poets (Merdipoeta!). This expression shows clearly, how important music was to Luther.[97]

c) Hymnbook Preamble

If we regard the letter and the preface to the choir work, both seem to say approximately the same thing. Music is a gift of God and it excites the soul. In that it is identical to the effects of theology. With the Preamble to the Hymnbooks, which we now arrive at, comes a new aspect.

Up to the time of Luther, a choir usually performed the music in worship service. The average church member in the late middle-ages participated in the service only through their presence, without any congregational singing. The development of the Lutheran liturgy is worth the effort of a lecture itself. For our context it is important mentioning that Luther at first maintained the Mass in Latin. Only in 1526 did he publish the "German Mass", in which he revised the Latin Mass liturgy to correspond with his theology. He valued Latin very highly in particular for the youth.[98] However, one can see in the Pentecost narrative that the Holy Spirit avails itself of different languages. And so he recommends German for the Bible texts and the Liturgy. Above all, the texts should be sung in the psalm-tonal technique and the congregation should respond accordingly, for example by singing the "Agnus dei" (lamb of God) at communion,

97 WA 50, p. 369-374: "Who don't want to receive the music in that way, they are dignified to listen to music of shitting poets (merdipoeta) and the music of pigs." (Transl. U.S.) Luther reflects with the strange term "Merdipoeta" to the student Simon Lemnius. He published Pentecost 1538 poems in which he praises Luther's Catholic opponent Cardinal Albrecht.

98 WA 19, p. 73. "Thus I don't want to dispose the Latin language from the worship service, because I take care of the Youth." (Transl. U.S.).

or singing the Credo after the Gospel.[99] Here we see in the order of worship already that the congregation is to be included into the procedures of the Liturgy. To that purpose Luther encouraged hymns for the worship service. Accordingly in 1524 he produced the first Hymnbook, the so-called "Eight-song book" and in the same year the "Sacred hymnbook". In the preface of this early songbook Luther writes again that music is a creative gift of God and that the prophets and kings in the Old Testament praised God with it. He wanted, therefore to place music gladly into the service of God.[100]

The purpose of singing songs is described here not so much as emotional elevation, but is instead theologically and educationally founded. First the educational: The songs are there so that "the youth ... have something to replace the courting songs and songs of the flesh and instead learn something beneficial."[101] The songs are thus for learning the salvation. As for the theological rationale for singing, Luther supposed that it concerned not only the proper use of a God's gift, but was also as a means to proclaim the Gospel:

> "After that a few others and I brought together a small number of spiritual songs, in order to give those who have greater ability a good beginning and foundation, so that the Holy Gospel, which is now, through God's grace spreading again, will be driven forward and be brought again into wide circulation."[102]

The songs are to serve the proclamation of the Gospel, which is now again coming in "Schwank" – in wide circulation. By this Luther understands naturally, the freedom of the Christian. One is able to further develop this point: The liberation of the Christian through the Gospel is the foundation for a fulfilled use of the gift of singing.

99 WA 19, p. 73.

100 WA 35, p. 475, 2-5: "Also I don't have in mind that the Gospel knocks down all arts that they die away, how some clergy mean. But I want to give all arts in to the service to God, who had given and created them." (Transl. U.S.).

101 WA 35, p. 474, 20-475, 1 (Transl. U.S.).

102 WA 35, p. 474, 11-13 (Transl. U.S.).

And the opposite applies as well: Those who cannot sing freely are not truly freed by the Gospel. This comes from another preface for a Hymnbook, the so-called Bapst Hymnbook. The Leipzig printer Valentin Bapst published a Hymnbook one year before Luther's death in 1545. As an aside, let me point out that there is a similarity in name between the name of the printer "Bapst" and the "Pope" (who in German is known as the Papst). Luther remarks on it merrily: This Valentin Bapst has arranged the book cheerfully, so that the Roman Pope (germ. Papst), who brought howls, mourning and suffering, will experience a great collapse.[103] As for the question of the relationship between the Gospel and song, we already find those reasons in the preface, which we encounter in 1524, and the point we concluded from it.

> "Then God made our hearts and courage joyous, by his dear Son, whom he gave to us for the deliverance from sin, death and the devil. Who earnestly believes this cannot help himself, he must sing about it with joy and with delight, so that others will also hear it and come to Christ. If one does not want to sing and speak of it, that is an indication, that one does not believe and belong to the joyous New Testament, but instead belongs under the old, lazy and dreary Testament."[104]

Singing is thus the test of the faith. If the Gospel redeems a person, then he can sing. If he cannot sing, the Gospel did not redeem him. And further, the singing serves to retell of this liberating faith. Missionary and theological thoughts flow together in this preface from Luther. It is in the connecting with the Gospel that the crux of the great value of music lies. The Gospel, of which he speaks here, is the Gospel of the cross of Jesus Christ. With that he is bound to experience the "merry changes", which justify humans before God,

---

103 WA 35, p. 477, 15-19 (Transl. U.S.).

104 Ibid., p. 477, 6-13 (Transl. U.S.).

without anything to do for it.[105] In this Gospel of the cross God is present through faith. And this faith meets the existence and lets the living being sing merrily. Applying the doctrine and the concept of the justification of Sinners in its practical effect to the context of music is not a later interpretation. Luther himself says clearly in the Leipziger Disputation (1519):

> "Cantare domino non semper est laetari et gaudere, immo canticum novum est canticum crucis." - "Singing to the Lord is not always being happy and joyous, on the contrary the new song is a song of the cross."[106]

In this respect singing is an effect of the new freedom that humans experience through the cross of Christ. Humankind receives liberation through faith, without having to do anything for the Lord, in order to earn it.

In closing we take a look at Luther's theological standpoint concerning music and thus we can retain the following aspects:

- music is a gift from God.
- music has a psychological effect. It makes the heart merry and moves it.
- music improves the proclamation of God's word and is a melody of the word of God, as is seen in the Bible among the prophets and kings.
- music serves in teaching the youth.

---

105 WA 10, 3, p. 356, 21-30. With category of the "merry change" (admirable commercium) Luther expresses the salvation of Christ in the sense of the doctrine of justification. "Hence then comes the wonderful change that Christ gives himself and his goods for the faith. And he takes the heart and what belongs to him. But what is in Christ? Innocence, piety, justice, beatitude and the best. Because Christ has overcome sin, death, hell and the devil. It happens for all, who understands, who firmly believes and trusts, that he will become in Christ Jesus a conqueror of sin and death, hell and devil. And also the innocence of Christ will become his innocence, likewise the piety of Christ, his holiness and salvation. And all what in Christ is, everything is in a faithful heart with Christ." (Transl. U.S.).

106 WA 2, p. 333, 25 (Transl. U.S.).

– music, particularly singing, is an indication of deliverance by the Gospel of the cross. Insofar music is immediately second to the theology, which proclaims this.

With this appraisal it is clear that Luther not only composed his own songs, but also gave practical recommendations for music in the service of worship. In the "German Mass" he recommends:

"For the sake of the simple people and the young people one must read, sing, preach, write and compose, and if it would be helpful I wouldn't hesitate to let all the bells ring and all the organs pipe and let everything that can make a sound do so."[107] Later he also writes: "Habemus organa propter iuventutem, We have an organ because of the youth – just as one would give children apples and pears."[108]

We come now to Luther's theological comparison between pictures and music and try to gain a perspective for our purpose here today.

1.3 Comparison of pictures and music in the works of Luther - principles of a Gospel-based art

It is already clear that Luther held music in higher esteem than the visual arts. But, exactly where do we see the commonalities and the differences? The commonalities exist, as far as I see, in the evaluation of art as God's gift and in its didactical use.

- Both music and painting are human works, in which humans can make use of their gifts. One can use these to praise God. One can also abuse them in relation to God. That would be what is meant by the "worldly courting songs" and in the false depictions of religious images, which corresponded to the medieval Catholic teachings.
- Both, art and music have a great educational importance. Music has as its target audience in the maturing youth. Painting's target audience consists of the simple people and

107 WA 19, p. 73 (Transl. U.S.).

108 WA 46, p. 452, 5 (Transl. U.S.).

> the so-called "common man". What both groups have in common is their entitlement to grow in the faith.

The differences between art and music, as far as I concern are in three aspects, namely in the Biblical foundation, the psychological effects and their relationship to the Doctrine of Justification.

1) Biblical foundation: If one goes through the Bible, it is easy to find positive statements about music. About the visual arts hardly good is said. This is also reflected in Luther's writings. On the question of the use of pictures he had to argue with the Carlstadt's literal interpretation of a prohibition of pictures. During evaluation of music it was easy for him to refer to the prophets or David, the Biblical singer-king. But, these different Biblical references are not only connected with the source as such, but also with our second aspect, the psychological effect.

2) Psychological effect: In the picture controversy Luther strived to differentiate between the object of the work of art and the beholder. Which religious meaning a human attaches to a work of art, is a personal matter. In the explanation of the didactical function of the visual arts, he renounces an emotive effect from the pictures, in comparison to how the medieval tradition treated it. It is completely different with music. Luther abandons a clear separation between object and subject, which was induced in the picture question due to the controversy. He focuses here much more on the direct effect of the artistic object of music on the psyche of humans. Music can make merry, create a sad mood, spread calmness and peace, just as the word of God can. Humans cannot therefore extract themselves from the effect of the music, in the same way they cannot extract themselves from the word of God. The comparison between music and theology culminates finally in the third aspect, the relationship to the theology of the cross.

3) Relationship to the Doctrine of Justification through Faith: There is nothing comparable here to the enquiry regarding pictures. Music and congregational singing are not only expressions of the Good News of redemption through the Gospel. The music itself serves the proclamation and personal meditation of the Doctrine of

Justification, for example, when Luther calls a new song, "the song of the cross" in the Leipzig Disputation.

The stronger effect of music on humans and its value in the context of the proclamation of the message of justification through faith naturally have their foundations in Luther's biography. He was himself a musician. He was an inspired singer and instigator of congregational singing. There is, however, still another reason for the higher appreciation of music.

Visual arts and congregational singing differ in the degree of participation. Luther had differentiated between beholder and picture. That was possible because the vision remained external. While singing a song one temporarily internalises the melody and the text. This describes participation at another level. If one wants to get right to the point, then the difference between visual arts and singing, as seen in Luther's works, is in the difference between reception aesthetics and performing utterances. The picture stands before the eyes, and is therefore outside. The spoken word is taken into the mouth, and so it enters inside. As a result of mixing this temporary community performance of words that belong partly to others and partly to your own, the song reaches a missionary and faith-deepening dimension. The newer religion didactics discovered long ago, that a temporary utterance of religious forms could lead to a learning experience.[109] This concept was called "performance-didactics". And one can, basically, expand this to the area of mission and the service of worship, when it comes to the question of congregational singing. Nowhere else are people more completely brought into the community experience as in active participation in congregational singing. The faith is strengthened. Luther was aware of that, without needing such conceptual contortions. Congregational singing is an indication of deliverance through Christ, and in its proclamation-function, singing frees. One can see how important the active participation in congregation singing was to him in 1529, 5 years after the introduction of the Hymnbooks. He

109 Silke Leonhard, Thomas Klie, Schauplatz Religion Grundzüge einer performativen Religionsdidaktik, Leipzig 2003.

is indignant about the fact that the slow-acting Wittenbergers did not yet know all the songs by heart, since they were more or less the biblia rudium - the Bible for the simple people.[110]

Finally, towards the end, we return to our starting question: Aren't there more important things to do in the work of the church? Certainly there are, as we can see when we look at the social misery around us. But addressing only the question of social hardship does not exhaust the task of mission. But rather, mission should be a communication of the Gospel in order to strengthen the faith. This can happen in social work and in shaping awareness. In the centre, however, stands as the celebration of faith, the celebration of the promise of the Gospel. Music helps us in doing this. It promotes an experience of community when the congregation is singing. The individual thereby tests the traditional and new modes of expression of faith in his specific life situation.

In closing, let me say a few sentences about the relationship between traditional and modern in music. Naturally, you inherited a treasure-trove of Hymns from the missionaries. Naturally, you have found your own new Hymns. It is a task for each generation to find a balance in the cultural manifestation of the Gospel. The Gospel of the free grace of God will always be proclaimed in a specific cultural form. In his time, Luther had taken up well-known songs and provided his own texts. He also invented new melodies. That is a task for every generation in every culture. Both belong together, the roots of the culturally specific expression of the Gospel and the search for new ways, the new song, that we as Christians are called to sing in light of our joyous deliverance. Thus, you sing the old ways, the Bhajans and other new ones, with drums or here in Ranchi with the organ. Each generation must negotiate this balance. But a safe criterion is handed to us: the new song is the song of the cross - canticum novum est canticum crucis.

---

110 WA 29, p. 44,14.

2. The Liturgy of the Gossner Church

In 2007, I had the honour to inaugurate an organ in Ranchi.[111] I followed the worship very attentively and thought I could have been travelling back to the 19th century. I do not mean this in a negative way. I was impressed because I met a liturgy that belongs in my home country to the 19th century and which has an exciting history. I was told that there exists a liturgical commission at Gossner Evangelical Lutheran *Church* (GELC) deliberating on the form of the liturgy. So, as a church historian I have started to trace the development of the liturgy. The following paper is meant to be a humble contribution to your contemporary cogitations. Together with you, I would like us to travel backwards in time and start by looking first at what the German sources tell us about the liturgy of the Gossner Church, secondly, how this liturgy developed, and thirdly and finally, I would like to offer some impetus for your further discussions.

2.1 The origin of the liturgy of the GELC – German sources

The missionaries that founded your church came mainly from Prussia. When they worshipped they used a form familiar to them, the Prussian order of service (Preussische Agende). Today one has to state that they implemented their own culture of worship without developing a liturgy suitable for the Adivasi. With the exception of

111 Lecture was held 1st Nov. 2008.

the musical work of Nathanel Tuyu, who was ordained in 1864 and who adapted many Bhajans for the Christian worship it was mainly European and Anglican traditions that dominated the liturgical culture of the developing church. One could discuss in which relationship culture and Gospel stand in the mission. But, one has to be cautious about which measures are to be used when judging the early history of the liturgy of the GELC. Did the missionaries have the possibility to create their own liturgy, one that was appropriate for the mission field? This question needs to be considered keeping in mind the influences of their time and the context within which their thinking developed.

Apart from these general thoughts on the origin of the liturgy, it is difficult to detect in the sources the exact point of decision as to when and how the "Preussische Agende" was made the order of service for the GELC. The few sources, we could find, concerning the liturgy of the GELC are general descriptions of the worship. As the sources for these descriptions are difficult to access, they have been included here in this paper.

1. Ludwig Nottrott: On the occasion of Johannes Evangelista Gossner's 100th birthday in 1873 Ludwig Nottrott published a description of the Gossner Mission in India that he called "Pictures from Missionary Life".[112] Herein, he first introduces the language and culture of the Adivasi of Chotanagpur to the German reader. Afterwards he outlines the history of the mission. He gives an account of the foundation of the first station Bethesda here in Ranchi, of the uprising in 1857 and finally he covers the division of some missionaries from the mission field of the Gossner Mission in Chotanagpur in 1868. Two of them were the missionaries Friedrich and Heinrich Batsch, who felt unable to accept a statute that ordered the sending of annual financial reports to the board (Kuratorium)

112 Ludwig Nottrott: Die Gossnersche Mission unter den Kohls. Bilder aus dem Missionsleben, Halle 1874. Ludwig Nottrott was the Brother of Alfred Nottrott, the famous missionary and principal of Gossner Mission in India. Ludwig published his description of the Adivasi church using the reports and letters of his brother while Alfred in India didn't know about his publishing activities of his brother.

of Gossner Mission in Berlin.[113] Lastly, he describes the mission stations. He begins this part with a general report on the spiritual life including an episode about the worship. It is, as far as I know, the oldest description of the worship of the GELC.

> "It is Sunday morning. […] The bells are ringing for the Church service. In a colourful queue they follow the call of the bells so that the church is soon filled. The men sit on the right, the women on the left. Then everyone kneels and with their heads bowed to the ground they say their initial prayer. The sounds of the organ, or if it is lacking of the reed organ, sweeps through the house of God. The simple Kohl hearts start to feel wonderfully festive. […] With enthusiasm they sing along to the melody of the hymn that is prompted to them verse by verse so that even the illiterate can join in. The singing is not always beautiful, but the heartiness replaces the beauty of the voices. The Kohls love to sing. That is why there is a lot of singing during the worship. – Then the organ quietens and Rev. Saheb steps forward in front of the altar, which consists of a beautiful draped table decorated with the Bible and candleholders. He holds in his hand the written book of the order of service that is essentially very similar to the Prussian order of service. Thus, the order of the liturgy is nearly the same as ours in Germany. Only the very different participation of the congregation astonishes us. They say aloud together the confession of sins, Creed and Lord's Prayer. A psalm after the confession of sins and the epistle is read in turn by the preacher and the congregation – a verse each. […] It sounds deeply moving when the whole congregation says aloud together each 'Amen' that appears in the liturgy."[114]

113 For this topic see also the paper "Social Movement of the Adivasi during the 19th century in Chotanagpur as reflected in German Sources" in this book, especially the part 2.3.b Division of Mission.

114 Ibid, p. 275f.

In this description, we already come across an adapted usage of the "Preussische Agende". It is readjusted to the missionary situation. When considering the differences in service, Nottrott suggests that the written book of order of service was "almost" completely the order of service familiar to him. He clearly names the differences: They are the collectively spoken parts and also the readings. Finally, he recognizes that the psalm has a special position: after the confession of sins (Confiteor). His conclusion is humiliating for the German reader: The congregation is more involved than in Germany. This is also underlined by Ludwig Nottrott in a work report of the Gossner Mission in India from 1888,[115] in which he gives an account of the festive culture of the worship and, by the way, also the formation of a brass band which was especially intended for open air mission festivals.[116] Ludwig Nottrott wrote:

> "Sunday service is always well attended, far better than the ones in the proselytizing German mother church."[117]

2. Another reference comes from the mission inspector Karl Heinrich Christian Plath. He visited the mission field in 1895. In that year the memorial stone, which stands in front of our Moderator's house, was inaugurated during the festivities marking

115 Ludwig Nottrot: Die Gossnersche Mission unter den Kohls. Die Arbeiten in den Jahren 1874-1887, Halle 1888.

116 Ibid, p. 146: "For dominating the thousands of guests of the feast especially while singing missionary Nottrott had already recognized at his first Mela (open air assembly) that a brass band was absolutely essential and that the two bugles he and his brother-in-law called for were insufficient. He ordered more instruments from Germany, but also got some from Ranchi where even missionary Häberlin had once years ago made a failed attempt to form a brass band. The training of the wind players was admittedly his business. But he managed to go to the Melas with ten wind players after several years of whom many owned their instruments, and hope remains that the Burju band will not stand alone for long." (Transl. U.S.).

117 Ibid, p. 136: The astonishment over the way worship is mentioned by visitors of the GELC today, but only after being asked insistently. It however has a long tradition as these more than 100 year old sources of Ludwig Nottrott prove. (Transl. U.S.).

the 50th anniversary of the arrival of the missionaries. In this place the four missionaries were said to have pitched their tent. Plath not only describes the progress of the work at each of the mission stations, he visited, but also the stone's inauguration ceremony. On the worship however he only notes summarily: "Our worships in the Kohl's congregations follow the Lutheran form of the Prussian order of service. We also followed the order with this festivity."

This note not only mentions the order of service already referred to by Nottrott. It also reveals that the order of service was perceived as so binding that even on such an exceptional day of celebration, it was arranged according to the "Preussische Agende". This arrangement was followed despite the fact that there was no prescribed order of service or special order of service – *proprium* for such an event.

Let us summarize the news from the 19th century. The authors recognize the Prussian order of service in the Gossner Church. The actual starting point cannot be found in any of the available sources. The records indicate that the order of service was adapted for the special missionary situation on the one hand, but on the other hand had an unalterable validity. But, where did this form of worship come from?

2.2 The origin of the Prussian order of service

When the missionaries departed for Kolkata, the order of service, they carried with them, was only 20 years old. The order of service cannot be traced to a particular Lutheran source. It was rather a work of compromise. It was supposed to reunite the Reformed and the Lutheran form of service. Let me therefore briefly portray the situation.

The electorate Brandenburg had accepted the Reformation in 1540. Large parts of the new order of church were borrowed from a Roman Mass book.[118] That means the form of the catholic mass was initially maintained to a large extend. When the provost of Berlin Georg Buchholzer complained about this, Martin Luther briefly

118 Emil Sehling, Die Evangelischen Kirchenordnungen des XVI. Jahrhunderts, Vol. 3, Leipzig 1909.

commented, one may wander around the church with "fool's caps" and "tinkling" as often as one pleases[119] as long as the Gospel that is preached is pure and sincere. Only 50 years later a Lutheran form of worship was developed with the introduction of "Visitations- and Consistorialordnung" of 1570 that was binding for all teachers and pastors. Now it happened that the elector of Brandenburg John Sigismund (1572-1619) reoriented himself towards the reformed confession, which had taken place in the Netherlands, from personal as well as political considerations. Christmas 1613 he converted to the Calvinistic-reformed confession. This step caused fierce resistance under pastors and nobles of the country. About 200 controversial writings against the elector were published in the course of five years.[120] The elector's decision was uncommon since the reformed confession was legally not accepted in the Holy Roman Empire at this time. Therefore the principle that the ruler dictated the confession (cuius regio, eius religio) could not be applied. The following electors made a virtue out of necessity. There came into existence, for this period in history, an exemplary political religious tolerance. Already in his testament John Sigismund had noted that no one should be pressurized in matters of religion.[121] Thus, a liberal climate developed. Over a hundred years later king Friederich II even ordered the settlement of religious refugees (Catholics, Reformed and even Muslims): "All religions are equal and good and as long as those practicing them are honest people and wish to populate our

119 Martin Luther, Brief an Georg Bucholzer vom 4.12.1539, WA Br. Vol. 8, p. 624, nr. 3421.

120 Michael Beintker, Vom Bekenntniswechsel Johann Sigismunds bis zum Edikt von Potsdam, in: Günther Wirth (Ed.), Berliner Kirchengeschichte, Berlin 1987, p. 45.

121 Refers from February 5th 1615 in: Phillipp Gercken: Codex diplomaticus brandenburgensis, V. 7, Stendal 1782, p. 91. Christian Otto Mylius: Corpus Constitutionum, Part VI, 1 nr. 79, c. 260: "… that every person in our country can remain at Luthers doctrine and the invariable Augsburg Confession, which was delivered to the emperor Kark V. in the year 1530 … It should omit to be done neither compulsion nor urge, because the king does not want to rule the consciousness of his people." (Transl. U.S.).

land, may they be Turks or Pagans, we will build them mosques and churches. [...] Everyone shall become blessed as he pleases."[122]

Then, a dispute concerning the order of service of the church burst into this climate of intellectual and religious freedom. Every elector and king of Brandenburg since John Sigismund made efforts to organise a peaceful coexistence of the confessions. The rulers understood it as their obligation to bring together the representatives of the different religions. After all, they were responsible for the church administration, the so called "consistory". (That would be, as if the Central Council was an office of the Indian state.) In the 19th century Frederick William III (1770-1840) came to the throne. The territory of Prussia was widely extended. The king saw the necessity to publish the new order of service for the church because he noted a decline of the religious rites and worship. It was indicated that parents stopped baptizing their children.[123] Even the language of the worship was perceived as antiquated so that the attendance at worship particularly in the cities faded. Other reasons for the declining of worship were the diversity of the order of service and confessional diversity:

- The diversity of the order of service in the age of Enlightenment: It was attempted in this period to establish forms of religion, which were logically deducible. For example: The sermon became an explaining lecture about moral issues. They try to explain the biblical stories of wonders with natural phenomenon. They spoke about liturgy as a "public religious cult". At the universities one was busy working on the liturgy and established that it had not changed for 200 years. Thus, several local orders of service developed around 1800 that significantly simplified the liturgy: After the initial hymn the offering was immediately

122 Letter from 22nd June 1740.

123 Royal Rescript on the decline of religiosity from 14th February 1802, p. 287-301 printed in: Erich Foerster, Die Entstehung der Preußischen Landeskirche unter der Regierung König Friedrich Wilhelms des Dritten nach den Quellen erzählt, Vol. 1, Tübingen 1905, p. 287-301.

collected. The sermon was followed by reading of a prayer. Each part of the liturgy was explained in full, at least the parts that had not been omitted.[124]

- The question of confession: The different confessions in Prussia had a disparate method of worship. The king means standardizing the liturgy will overcome the diversity of confessions. A shared form of worship of Lutherans and Calvinists was thought to lead to a joint confession, a union. That is why the order of service was also called the "union order of service".

The king himself studied in-depth the problems of liturgy. He examined different reformed orders of service. He took the model of a Lutheran service as a basis and introduced reformed elements.[125] It would be too extensive to list every particularity. Let me just mention some parts:

- For example, Calvin used to open his worships with a sentence from the preliminary part of the Roman mass, the so called "Adjutorium nostrum": "Our help is in the name of the Lord, who made heaven and earth." (Ps. 124:8)
- The order of service instructed that the liturgy was to be celebrated at length at the beginning of the worship, while the sermon was placed at the end.
- Furthermore, the king had engaged a well known composer for the composition of the liturgical pieces: *Dimitri Bortinjanski* (1751-1825). Born in Ukraine, he became a disciple of the Italian composer Balthasare Galuppi in St.

124 Paul Graff, Geschichte der Auflösung der alten gottesdienstlichen Formen in der evangelischen Kirche Deutschlands bis zum Eintritt der Aufklärung und des Rationalismus, Vol. 2, Göttingen 1921/1939. If this really is to be judged as decay, remains questionable. Basically, it was the first time that a contemporary order of service – in fact a more radical one than in the Reformation – was created.

125 Walter Elliger, Die Evangelische Kirche der Union, ihre Vorgeschichte und Geschichte, Witten 1967, p. 49.

> Petersburg. He followed Galuppi to Italy and composed several operas in the Italian style. In 1779, he returned to Petersburg where he stayed till his death, a year after Johannes Evangelista Gossner had been forced to leave Petersburg.[126] Bortinjanski helped choral singing to flourish at the court of the Tsar, as the Prussian king recognized with envy. So the king, too, established a Russian choir in his residence (Alexandrowka), which was supposed to celebrate the songs and musics of Bortinjanski. In his concept of the order of service, which was first meant for the cathedral congregation in Berlin, the king planned that the liturgical pieces were to be sung by a choir.[127]

He spread his order of service among the pastors of his country with the intention to introduce it on the occasion of the tercentenary of the Reformation in 1817. The order of service caused a storm of protest. 191 leaflets and texts were published against the order of service. Friedrich Schleiermacher, the foremost theologian of Berlin, and the king had a feud against each other partly using anonymous texts. The main point of criticism was on the one hand the *ius liturgicum* (i.e., the right to change the liturgy). The king was entitled to pass church laws. That also included liturgical law. It had never been used before in this manner where the king as a layman created the order of service. On the other hand there was criticism that the liturgy would outweigh the sermon, that everything was to be sung by the choir (even in the congregations in the country), that liturgical

126 Bortinjanski composed the melody of the song "Ich bete an die Macht der Liebe", in English "How glorious is our Lord in Zion" which is also today sung in Sakhsi Bani. The song was published with the text of Gerhard Teestegen the first time in a songbook, which Father Johannes Gossner published together with Johannes Tscherlitzky at his time in Saint Peterborough. Johannes Evangelista Gossner, Sammlung auserlesener Lieder von der erlösenden Liebe, Leipzig 1925, No. 86. Johannes Evangelista Gossner, Choralbuch, Enthaltend die Melodieen zu der Sammlung auserlesener Lieder von der erlösenden Liebe und dem Schatzkästchen, Leipzig 1825, p. 62.

127 Walter Elliger, Die Evangelische Kirche der Union, p. 49.

elements of the communion, as for example the preface, even appear, when no communion is celebrated, that a uniform order of reading and sermon is prescribed, etc.

The king revised the liturgy. Regional orders of service were created and he reshaped the order of service in two versions, a Lutheran and a Reformed. The choral singing was optional. Then, in 1829, came the time when the order of service would be released and signed into law. This was to take place on the occasion of the jubilee of the Augsburg Confessions in 1830. All pastors had to sign the order of service.

Despite the revision several congregations saw this order of service as a sacrilege because of the mixing of the different confessions. Particularly in the Silesian congregations the resistance was fierce. In the first phase of the dispute two thirds of the pastors refused to accept the order of service. The theological faculty of the University of Breslau had fuelled the resistance. When the order of service became law a new church developed in Germany, the so called old Lutherans, and many disaffected people emigrated. Many Lutherans from Silesian villages tried their luck in Australia, where they took part at the foundation of the Australian-Lutheran Church.[128]

What does this walk through the history of the origin of the order of service mean for the order of service of the GELC? Let us summarize briefly: The order of service that the missionaries brought with them was originally expected to create a compromise among the confessions. It is the work of the king and his advisors. The hymns, and therefore also the ones you sing today, were written by the Russian composer Bortinjanski. The king had virtually imported them into his order of service. Though the order of service was based on a Lutheran model, many Christians in Brandenburg Prussia perceived that it was not Lutheran enough. Neither the Prussian king nor all the disputers were probably aware of the fact that the order of

128 Curt Schelenz, Kreis Züllichau Schwiebus, Frankfurt 1970. Schelenz describes basing on the chronicle remarks that Christians from the village Klemzig fled to Australia because of the new Prussian order of service. They founded a village nearby Adelaide, which still exists.

service gained a global dimension in the worldwide church through the missionaries.

What happened to the order of service in Germany? It had been already reworked at the end of the 19th century. In 1895, a revision of the Prussian order of service was published in which the strict thought of union was abolished. In it we find two forms of worship, a Lutheran and a Reformed. Again numerous regional orders of service were released which reflected special local traditions. The Prussian order of service became a kind of archetype for these local orders of service. Around 1930 another revision of the Prussian order of service was made. A fundamental novelty was that the *introitus* was followed by several psalms instead of an initial proverb, which were followed by the *Gloria patri*. In the end of the 1950s, another reform introduced new antiphonal anthems and rejected the music of Bortinjanski.

2.3 Inspiration for the present

The eventful development and history of the Prussian order of service illustrates that the form of the order of service and liturgy are temporally relative. In the formation of the order of service and the liturgy of worship one basically tried to follow two principles.

- One principle is the tradition. A standardized form was supposed to create a connection between protestant Christians and bind them together.
- The other principle is the adjustment. The adjustment of the liturgical form to the local situation of the congregation, their language and their time, was thought to serve the adoption of the Christian faith. This was only possible because the traditional form have no truth revealing character like for example the understanding of liturgy in the Orthodox or Catholic Church implies.

Both aspects seem to differentiate substantially and therefore seem to come into conflict with each other again and again in the course of history. But, there exists a connecting question behind both principles. What is our identity today as members of the congregation of Christ? The term "identity" implies that it is something durable through time, which however, every generation has to adopt anew and continue with.

Therefore, a cultural and anthropological argument will be laid out here. Liturgy supports the cultural memory.[129] Adoption of the liturgical form serves the purpose of envisaging a contradictory presence in the changing present time, to which we belong in all totality. That may sound complicated. You can simplify it to the metaphorical phrase: The liturgy is a stable house throughout changing times. The Egyptologist Jan Assman coined the term "cultural memory". Concerning religion he means that the identity of a religion is bound to an extraterritorial point of memory in the past. This can be well understood in the commemoration of the Jewish Pesach. The family reminds itself of the origin of its religion in the desert. In a family ritual the youngest son asks the father to tell the story of the exodus. It is recalled and experienced in the process of narration. Basically this phenomenon of recollection and the related building of identity can be transferred to ritual actions, the liturgy, the reading of the Bible and also prayer. Through a specific form of recollection, a faithful person, together with the social community of the church establish themselves in an extraterritorial point, not in a present point of time. But, the use of recollection and bringing to mind of a different extraterritorial and super-temporal point out of time now results in an actual development. That means the principle of tradition will only survive, if there is the other principle, namely the actual development and also adaptation of the tradition to the actual life situation. Thus, both belong together in the execution of liturgy: the super-temporal of tradition and the adaptation to the current circumstances of life.

129 Jan Assmann, Religion und kulturelles Gedächtnis, München 2000, p. 67. The book is translated: Jan Assmann, Religion and Cultural Memory: Ten Studies (Cultural Memory in the Present) transl. by Rodney Livingstone, Stanford University Press 2006.

Maybe the interaction of tradition and adaptation can well be demonstrated by means of a biblical story. When Elijah went up to heaven, he and his disciple Elisha arrived at the River Jordan (2 Kgs. 2:1-14). "Elijah smites the waters with his mantle so that they could walk over on dry ground." Elijah goes up "by a whirlwind into heaven" (V. 11). But, he left his mantle for Elisha. Elisha turns back, goes back to Jordan, smites the waters with the mantle, he has inherited, and reaches the other bank on dry ground. Elisha is not alone. He has got the mantle and the prophet's spirit.

Liturgy is quite similar to the mantle in the story. We have got it from our fathers. If you wear and pass on a mantle, you will have to sew on a button every now and then or renew a seam. In doing so you adapt the mantle, you make it fit you. But it stays the same mantle. Let us apply this to liturgy. It, too, stays the same. But we are called to work on it, to cautiously adjust it to our language and time. Liturgy wants to be worn and adjusted by us like a mantle and then we can pass it on to our children. With what can they save themselves? With what can they warm themselves?

All three aspects, which play a part while thinking about liturgy flow together in this story. We have got the identity because we find ourselves born into a tradition; We are at the same time bearers of this tradition; And we and the following generations are responsible to adopt the tradition. The basic questions that emerge while thinking about liturgy are therefore: What is my identity? And how do I ensure a vigorous adoption here and now, so that I preserve the heritage of the saving and serving mantle? We save the mantle by adapting the liturgy, so that the mantle will save, protect and warm us in the changing times.

Section 3

Social Freedom

1. Mission as Misunderstanding – An Observation on Conversion Processes

To be a part of God's Mission means to participate at a global process of transformation of the Gospel.[130] Christ is speaking to the world and the Gospel becomes different cultural expressions. But, what is at the beginning of the faith when the Gospel changes its cultural expression in another context? This leads me to analyse the existing reports about the first conversion in the Indian Gossner Family to find out, how far in the beginning of faith, inculturation was already present. I would like now to present the result of these thoughts to you.

As a first step, we will take a closer look at the question as to why it is not very easy to explain the actual beginning of belief, then we will turn to the history of the conversion of the Oraon, and finally we will draw some lessons from our deliberations.

1.1 The theological problem of conversion

In the theological school where I studied in Germany, it was not easy to talk about the beginning of faith. It was during my first visit here in Ranchi that I became aware of this. "Are you also happy to be a Christian?" It was at an official reception in honour of my first visit to the GELC. The man had simply approached me. Besides the fact that it was unusual in the Indian cultural context to address the

130 Lecture was held on 21st Jan. 2012.

"mission director" directly and not through the church hierarchy and bishops, I was frankly surprised by this question. "Yes", I responded somehow embarrassed. And avoiding a genuine response, I asked: "And you yourself?" The young man answered: "I am really happy since I do not have to be afraid of death anymore; afraid of the Bongas (spirits) intervening in my life and oppressing me. He continued by asking "And from which Bongas have you been freed?" Now the conversation became personal and very interesting, because it touched the centre of the question from what had the Christian faith set me free and which spirits and powers frightened me.

Particularly in Germany, within the circles of the established churches, we are not used to openly discuss questions relating to the relevance and beginning of our personal belief. In my view, there are two reasons for this: One can be found in the confessional doctrine of the Lutheran faith which leads to an individualisation (1.1), the other one is caused by the wide spread theology of the Missio Dei (1.2).

Sola fide

It is the merit of the reformation that it has set the question of individual belief and the following personal liberation back on the agenda. In the view of Luther and Melanchthon, the "fiducia", the personal confidence in God, is the main aspect of faith. On the other hand, a mere knowledge of the Christian faith based on historical facts or on the merit of Christ, is not sufficient.[131] The acceptance of the faith as fiducia, as my confidence, is only reasonable under the presumption that the Gospel is already present in the world and that it can be known and is being propagated. Therefore, the reformers had to distinguish between two conditions for the beginning of belief: one the universal coming of God into the world through his incarnation in Jesus Christ; and the second, the entering of God into

131 Especially in the Apology of Augsburg Confession Melanchthon criticized this position. BSLK, p. 162, 29-163, 25; Art.IV, 9-12. Full Text is available: http://bocl.org?AP+IV.

each individual personally.[132] This differentiation was crucial for the reformers, since it was only a firm personal trust or faith, which could guarantee salvation. It was only on this basis of personal belief that justification was possible (sola fide). Personal belief was a result of the grace of God, which at the same time functioned as justification. This concept, however, was already criticised in the period of reformation by its own representatives, such as the early Muentzer, because in cases of counselling "it did not teach those, whom were willing to believe, how to come into the faith".[133] Nevertheless, there was now a distinction to be considered within the mission to distinguish between (i) the witness (suasion) of man talking about the coming of God into the world, and (ii) the inner conviction (persuasion) as the work of God within the individual. This means, the personal belief is a result of an act by God himself. It is God who is convincing about what man can only witness with simple words. The confidence in the truth of the Gospel is a present from God to the individual. By saying this, Luther laid the foundation for a modern image of human beings, which was in line with the age of enlightenment and resulted mainly in an intellectual liberty of conscience and tolerance. The liberating perception that belief is an action taken by God within the individual, resulted in the individualisation of faith.

Missio Dei

The perception of belief as a movement of God was extended in the 20th century by the Missio-Dei-theology mainly established by

---

132 Melanchthon defines in his book Loci communis (Common Places in Theology or Fundamental Doctrinal Themes – Luther said: Next to the holy scripture there is no better book), a protestant Dogmatic Theology which was commonly known for three hundred years: "Fides et assentiri universo verbo Dei nobis propositio adeoque et promossioni gratuitae reconciliationis ... estque fiducia misericordia Dei" Melanchthon Loci, CR 21, 744.

133 Siegfried Bräuer/ Hans Jürgen Görtz, Art. Thomas Müntzer, in: Martin Greschat (Hg.), Gestalten der Kirchengeschichte, Bd. 5 Reformationszeit I, Stuttgart 1984, p. 338.

Karl Hartenstein.[134] Mission, or "sending", was understood as a Trinitarian concept: God the father sends his son Jesus Christ. Father and son send the Holy Spirit to reconcile the world. Christ says: "Like the father sent me, so I send you" (John 20:21). Through this Trinitarian foundation of mission, which was also welcomed by the orthodox and catholic churches, limitations and lopsidedness would be avoided. Mission is no longer a work of the church, but the church subordinates itself under the mission of God, the commitment of God to the world. God himself is the subject of the mission. It is He, who acts and spreads the Christian faith. With this direction of thinking from above, what already appeared within the criticisms of Muentzer against Luther was neglected, that is to ask how people come to have a personal belief, how they themselves become personal witnesses and carriers of the mission.[135]

The theology of Luther as well as the Missio-Dei-theology, both respect the difference between human witness and divine action in the process of missionary action. It is obvious that by doing so the danger of mechanising the missionary witness is avoided. The mystery of faith, its contingency, is being protected. What would happen if we knew how people come to believe in God? Could a faith created by some sort of human means still be called "faith"? In the Letter to the Hebrews, the well-known words are written: "Now faith is the substance of things hoped for, the evidence of things not seen." (Heb. 11:1). Faith taken on trust always has this mysterious dimension of the uncontrollable.

On the other hand, this notion of the mystery of faith should not lead to the situation whereby no statements or just vague statements on its birth in man are possible. The task, therefore, is to describe the origin of faith as a "relational" act by maintaining the distinction between human witness and God's action. The question "How does faith begin?" thus has to be asked against the background of the

134 Peter Samuel Jost, Karl Hartenstein und die missio Dei, Zeitschrift für Missionswissenschaft, 3-4/ 2010, pp. 305-324.

135 Heinrich Balz, Der Anfang des Glaubens, Theologie des Glaubens und der jungen Kirchen, Erlangen 2010, p. 173.

difference between human witness (suasion) and divine persuasion. Equipped with this distinction, we now want to turn to the question: How does faith begin in the first conversion?

1.2 The conversion of the first Oraon

From 1836, onwards Johannes Evangelista Gossner trained and sent missionaries into various regions of the world. He was concerned about the spiritual counselling of the settlers in America and Australia as well as the conversion of the so-called gentiles.[136] With this vision, Emil Schatz, Friedrich Batsch, August Brandt and Theodor Jahnke were sent to North-East India, to the region of "Chotanagpur". When in 1845 they erected their tent in Ranchi right in the centre of Chotanagpur[137], they did not foresee that it would take five years until their first "mission success" under the casteless Oraon would materialise. The German brothers corresponded with Berlin forwarding the request to transfer them to a different mission field, where successes would be achieved more quickly. Gossner responded: "Whether the Kohls convert or not, this shall not be your concern; if they do not want to accept the word, they shall hear about their decision when they are judged it to their own judgment. You shall just pray and continue preaching, and we ourselves shall also pray."[138] Gossner in his reply recalls the distinction between human witness (suasion) and persuasion by God described earlier on. The acceptance of the Gospel cannot be in the hands of the missionaries. It must be prayed for. In fact, the long aspired impact by God materialises, with a remarkable learning process on all sides as we will see.

In those days, it was unusual that Europeans, Sahibs, or Hindus respectively would share a meal with casteless people. This, however, was the defining moment for the first conversion as the missionaries

136 Herrmann Dalton, Johannes Gossner. p. 393. Walter Holsten,: Johannes Evangelista Gossner. p. 48-156.

137 Walter Holsten, p. 235f. Herrmann Dalton, Johannes Gossner, p. 383f.

138 Ludwig Nottrott, Die Gossnersche Mission unter den Kolhs, Halle 2nd. Ed. 1895, p. 184.

reported in a letter. Emil Schatz wrote to Berlin on August 1st, 1850:

> "June 9th was an important day for us. ... Kesu and his son in law Bandhu-Gurha and Neumann have been baptised today; ... Our dear brothers out of the Koles have been seeking for a long time, following all the Hindu ways, but they did not find the peace that they were seeking. ... They came (to us) with amazement and joy, but did not like the fact that they were sinners and would become sinners; they perceived themselves as heroes of pureness. Hence, they left again. However, they could not resist coming back. And so they came back and forward for the past two years. All of a sudden they confessed to be great sinners. Now they wanted to seek the truth seriously. ... One Sunday morning, they came for the service. When everybody left at the end – they stayed – we talked to them; and they stayed. Since we held our English service at 12 o'clock, we asked: 'Would you like to stay? 'Yes, we stay.' So we left them sitting there. – They realised then that we on our part would not do anything else other than: singing, praying, reading, preaching, and that we would not use any Hokuspokus (magical tricks). They were very impressed by this. ... After the service with us, they agreed to eat a meal with us. This was now what we did. Never will we forget this. ... We had the meal in front of us – we prayed and in God's name: they were conquered. (The fence between the castes was torn down by this common meal; the most difficult part was overcome.) Since we did not have any reason to doubt the pureness of their step and they complained about our hesitation, we baptised them into the death of Jesus. May the Lord have written their names in the book of life."[139]

139 Biene, 1851, No. 1, p. 3f. (Transl. U.S.).

This report describes how God persuades and how one can misunderstand one another at first sight in a human manner. It is because two horizons of understanding meet each other.

a) The missionaries: The missionaries expect a confession to Christ and, even more important, a confession to be "great sinners". This "they did not like". The missionaries were living in the theology of the 19th century. For them, the question was not really whether the recognition of sin is possible without forgiveness of sin as is discussed in modern theology. For them, the notion of superiority of their religion was crucial. The indigenous religion or the Hindu religion in itself was a sin. This had to be realised first.

b) The Adivasi: The other horizon of understanding was that of Kesu and his friends. They are fascinated by the message of the equality of brothers and sisters originating in the Gospel. They are fascinated by the fact that Christianity does not have a concept of a double religion with a sacred area behind the common religion. On the contrary, they discovered: The Sahibs did nothing different in their service than they did in the service with them, which is preaching the word, prayers and songs. Finally, the common meal broke the barrier, since it was unusual for the Sahib to eat together with an Adivasi.

Both horizons of understanding do not match. One of them aims at realising sin, the other one at the equality of sisters and brothers. How at all could they understand each other? Maybe, one can ask even more pointedly: Have Batsch and Kesu simply misunderstood each other, since Batsch aimed at the conversion of sinners and Kesu was looking for social acceptance? It was lucky that there was this misunderstanding between the missionary and the recipient. Possibly this was even a precondition for the mission to be a "success". Anyway, a gap in communication becomes evident and was discovered by both sides. It is interesting to notice that this phenomenon of a beneficial misunderstanding or a communicative gap in the *conversion* of Kesu is not an exception, as modern mission theology teaches us.

1.3 The communicative gap

In the development of African theology, a useful distinction has been introduced. It is helpful for developing independent theological concepts in Africa. One observes two levels for communicating the Gospel. There is the historical communication of the message by the missionaries on the one hand and the indigenous reception and cultural interpretation on the other. As for the human witness of the white missionaries the term "transmission" was established which means conveying or bringing. The missionaries brought the Gospel. The receiving of the Gospel was called "assimilation".[140] This meant roughly adjusting or even adapting. This concept developed by Lamin Sanneh and Kwame Bediakoh extends that of Andrew Walls who perceived in this process of assimilation the incarnation of faith in different cultural manifestations[141] and a conversion (!) by Christ in "location, thoughts, relations and philosophies where he never was before".[142]

Although this consequence contradicts the occidental perception of ubiquity and does not necessarily have to be drawn, this distinction still facilitates the appreciation of the beginning of faith as a unique history of inculturation. In this way, the African theology was able to retreat from the reproachful colonial mission. It is because of this assimilation that a new Gospel Light could shine in a new context, which was previously, obscured in a human and often critical transmission. This is how conversion stories can let the richness of the Gospel appear in a new bright light. The one light of the Gospel contains various differing contextual lights.

Following this distinction it becomes evident that in the process of communicating the Gospel: The truth of the recipient is different from that of the messenger. It is never identical. This distinction can easily be noticed in the story of the conversion of Kesu. The

140 Kwame Bediakoh, Christianity in Africa, The Renewal of a Non-Western Religion, New York 1997, pp. 205-207.

141 Ibid., p. 109.

142 Ibid., p. 165.

motives of transmission and assimilation are clearly distinct from one another:

- For the missionaries, repenting and renouncement of the old life was a precondition: One has to confess one's sins. The transmission motive is: the repenting sinner receives God's grace. In order to receive grace, first repentance has to be shown and sins must be confessed.
- The Oraon want to belong to Christianity, because the Christian faith establishes equality between sisters and brothers. When the Oraon realised the social bursting power of the Gospel, "they were conquered". The assimilation motive, therefore, consisted of the social equality shining through the liberating word of God.

We have formulated the task of describing the birth of faith as relational act while respecting the distinction of human witness and God's activity. In my view, this distinction is maintained by accepting a gap between transmission and assimilation in the communication process of the dissemination of the faith. It is in this gap, which in human eyes looks like a misunderstanding where the Holy Spirit operates. He creates a culturally acceptable understanding of the Gospel. This can be observed in the beginning of the history of the GELC in the first conversion. Hence, already in the beginning of the history of the GELC the motive of an indigenous theology of the Adivasi can be seen, which we nowadays meet in many forms through the interpretation of the social relevance of the Gospel. The history of the beginning of faith in the GELC should encourage you to further develop an Adivasi-Theology of your own. It is as old as the Gospel in Chotanagpur.

The Adivasi theology is part of the worldwide light of Christ. Let us continue our communication about the Gospel even if and when we sometimes do not fully understand one another with our human words – so let us continue misunderstanding each other, the Holy Spirit will work in the gap!

2. Social movement of the Adivasi during the 19th century in Chotanagpur as reflected in German sources[143]

The Missionaries were able to report to the Mission father Johannes Evangelista Gossner in Berlin in 1850, five years after their arrival, about the first conversion of a group of adult Adivasi. It is obvious in this report that there is a communicative gap between the missionaries and the Oraon in their understanding of the Gospel.[144] In the process of first conversion it is obvious that the Missionaries and the Adivasi had a different understanding on the social implications of the truth of the Gospel. The misunderstandings based on these distinct interpretations and the resulting differences, would accompany the work of the missionaries throughout the 19th century. The difference is in the following years apparent in the question of land. The debate is whether to understand the Gospel as liberation of the heart or as liberation from social oppression.

Before describing the perspective of the missionaries to the question of land property and its social relevance I will describe in brief the background of the conflict.

143 Lecture was held at 31st October 2014 at the Triennial Conference of Church History Association of India.

144 Cf. the Paper "Mission as Misunderstanding – An Observation on Conversion Processes" in this book.

2.1 The question on land in Chotanagpur

When the first missionaries began their work in Chotanagpur, they were aware of the difficult social situation of the local indigenous peoples. The underlying problem was that of land ownership. According to the tradition of the tribal people the land belonged to the person who had originally cultivated it. He was called "Khuntkattidar" or "Bhuinar". This ownership of the founder's family was maintained even when the land was given to other families to cultivate.[145] These families had only the right to the crop yield from the land.

The separation between right of ownership and right of use remained even when a kingdom developed in Chotanagpur. The reasons for the emergence of a kingdom are not exactly known. One reason may be that the Mundas as the Austro-asiatic tribe and Oraons as Dravidian tribe agreed to an external leader.[146] The Khuntkattidars were committed to respect the king and to serve him in his militia. This legal system was binding on all parties until the mid of 17th century when then the king claimed not only a part of the yield of the land, but laid claim to the land itself. Following the example of neighbouring Mogul rulers, he installed the so-called Zamindars (feudal lords) and so-called local Thikadars (tenant farmers). The king converted to Hinduism and with the help of his Brahmin lifted his Zamindars up into the second highest Hindu caste - the Kchatriyas (warriors). Therefore, they were endowed with special rights.[147] With this process Hindus migrated into the territories of the indigenous population in Chotanagpur.

Between the new masters and the indigenous population of the country arose conflicts over land ownership. The indigenous population took for granted that there was a separation of ownership and income rights. The tax collectors however tried to claim the

---

145 Sarat Chandra Roy, The Mundas and their Country, London 1970, p. 75. The term Khuntkattidar is used mainly regarding the land of the Mundas, the other tribes use the term "Bhuinari".

146 Helmut Borutta, Revolution für das Recht, Erlangen 1994, p. 47.

147 Ibid., p. 40.

land for themselves and their masters whenever there were cases of default on the payment of higher taxes. When the British took over the sovereignty of Chotanagpur in 1771, it was hard for them to solve the problem of land ownership. This was because they had to rely on translators, who worked as Hindus in favour of their masters. Unfortunately the British gave the Zamindars in 1809 official police rights. Thus, the indigenous people were without rights.[148] The taxes were continually increased, even the fruit of planted trees could be no longer picked by the people.[149] This led to a major revolt in 1831-32, in which 3000 Adivasi fought together, but they were no match for the military superiority of the British. The Adivasi leaders surrendered voluntarily.[150]

2.2 The question of land from the missionaries' perspective

The question of land ownership accompanied the missionaries from the beginning. However, as with other social questions, it was not a central theme for them as was already clear from their description of the first Adivasi conversion. Although, the missionaries revealed a change in their perception of the question on land in their communication with Berlin, their attitude was dominated by a continued theological distance to this issue. It was based on the Lutheran separation between the external and inner man. In Luther's book "On the freedom of a Christian" the Reformer postulated: "A Christian is a perfectly free lord of all, subject to none." The external man, however, continues to live in his (from God given) social position and therefore he is available as "a perfectly dutiful servant of all, subject to all." This idea is strengthened within the revival theology of father Johannes Gossner's in the 19th century. He was concerned during his mission with the "Gottseligkeit", the godliness of the inner man - of his heart. The missionaries' beliefs were deeply rooted in this way of thinking and we will see that we encounter this idea not only among

148 Suresh Singh, The Dust-storm and the Hanging Mist, Calcutta 1966, p. 5.

149 Sarat Chandra Roy, The Mundas and their Country, p. 113.

150 Helmut Borutta, Revolution für das Recht, p. 45.

them but also among the catechists whom they taught. But, how did they perceive the land question from their perspective?

The missionaries reported to their German homeland regularly through articles in the missionary magazine, the so-called "Biene auf dem Missionsfeld", "The bee in the mission field." Additionally there were a few scientific articles, which were published in the "Allgemeine Missionszeitschrift", "The general missionary magazine", which was founded 1874. In the following paper I would like to evaluate these sources, which deal mainly with the news sent to the German readers through the mission journal about the missionaries and their work. As far as I am concerned we can describe three distinct phases in the perceptions surrounding the land question:

a) Bishop Cotton and the silence of the missionaries

In spring of 1864 the Anglican Bishop George Edward Lynch Cotton visited the German mission in Ranchi. When he came out of the Christ Church a group of indigenous Christians comes up to him. They recognised him evidently as an officer of the British government and wanted to hand a petition to him. They requested that he should stand up for their rights on the land. The German missionary Friedrich Batsch, who accompanied the Bishop, took the petition out of their hand. He ripped up the petition in front of their eyes. This symbolic action is omitted from the articles in the mission journal, and thus concealed from the German reader. Instead of this they printed a letter from Bishop Cotton to the Chairman of the Gossner Mission General Superintendent Carl Büchsel. Bishop Cotton wrote that the mission should have stronger financial support and should possibly strengthen cooperation with the Anglican Church.[151] Three years later, in 1867, the readers of the magazine learnt through a detailed report by Friedrich Batsch about the land question and how great the burden was on the Adivasi caused by taxes and arbitrariness. He concludes his article:

151 Biene, 1864, No. 11, pp. 81-83.

> "Is the government doing nothing? Are there no courts in the country; is there no police? Yes, indeed, in abundance. But the British hear, see and talk about everything through the native agents who are not Kols, but Hindus and Muslims, and these sorts of people are, when it comes to greed, even worse than the Jagirdars and Thikedars. Here, lawsuits cost so much that there is hardly any way for the common man, to bring a case before the courts in order to uphold his rights. In the rare event that a Kol wins his case, it is unfortunately very difficult to enforce this achieved right."[152]

Batsch recognizes very accurately the difficult legal situation surrounding the Adivasi land question. But even here he conceals the essentials such as the encounter during the visit of Bishop Cotton.

The experience of arguing unsuccessfully in court and thereby losing a lot of money was made by a group of Adivasi a year earlier in 1866. A group of presbyters of the Mundas and the Uraons had collected money in the villages and sued in the Calcutta court against the arbitrariness of Tikardars. They had no success. The process, however, dragged on as this was in the interest of lawyers. Friedrich Batsch had strongly condemned these so-called "Calcutta-goers". He referred to them from the pulpit as "damned people". He even excommunicated them. This is only reported in 1874 by the young Missionary Thomas Jellinghaus, who wrote about these events in an article for the scientific reader in the General Missionary Magazine. Jellinghaus attended the church during the damnation of the "Calcutta-goers". How embarrassing this must have been for the young missionary is recognized in a footnote, in which he stated:

> "It has been denied in later public documents; but even then, as a new Missionary of only five months, I wrote the words of my inner outrage in my diary followed by;. "Deus

152 Biene, 1867, No. 12, p. 97f. (Transl. U.S.).

mihi causa tacendi poenam non dabit." (God let me not conceal the cause of their punishment.)[153]

Apart from the long article by Friedrich Batsch in the mission journal, where he concealed the excommunication of the land law activists, and his ripping up of the petition, only a few notes on the sufferings of Adivasi in connection with the land question can be found in the period up to 1868. The relative silence on the question of land marks the first phase of the mission. But change will come.

b) Division of Mission – the question of land becomes a subject

In 1868 there was a division between the German missionaries. Father Johannes Gossner had originally sent his missionaries to India without financial support. The missionaries were expected to live by their work as craftsmen and teachers in the mission field. The missionaries through donations from Germany, through protection of the British and through careful financial management, gradually acquired houses and land, and therefore, the mission agency in Berlin began to regulate the Indian mission field. They introduced mission statutes and regulated the ownership of the land of the mission. The conflict cannot in detail be described here. The older missionaries did not feel that they had been involved in drafting the mission order. Furthermore, sending Hermann Ansorge as an inspector to Ranchi offended them. Therefore, in the autumn of 1868 six missionaries declared their withdrawal from the Gossner Mission. Among them were the first missionaries Friedrich and Heinrich Batsch. They set up what in various sources was described as a so-called "Counter Mission", which they linked to the Anglican Church. For this purpose Bishop Milman ordained them again.[154] Their hope was to win over as many of the Adivasi as possible to their side.[155] The land question

153 Thomas Jellinghaus, Die Kolhs in Ostindien und ihre Christianisierung, in: Allgemeine Missionszeitschrift 1 (AMZ 1874), p. 256.

154 Biene 1869, No. 8, p. 65.

155 Biene 1869, No. 4, p. 28: So "the old missionaries were leading in their excitement to build a counter-mission in the heart of Ranchi, where they

seems to have been particularly suited to serving this purpose. The representatives of the "counter-mission" attempted, especially in the rural areas, to demonstrate that they had better options on offer for assistance because of their enhanced contacts with British officers. This led in some places to a situation of competitiveness. A report of missionary Jellinghaus about the Murumkela village located nearby to Gossnerpur/ Govindpur may serve as an example:

> "Four years ago, six Christian families were expelled by the Thikedar from the village Murumkela, three of these families are connect to the counter-mission and three to us. If the counter-missionaries tell people: come to us, we will help you - they often reply: Help first the displaced Murumkela Christians." Now people often asked: 'Who will be the first to move back to Murumkela, the Christians belonging to the old church, or those who are loyal to the British?' Our opponents had often met with the Thikedar, but in vain. Well I visited him, the evil enemy of Christians, and spoke to him in a very friendly way, he told me, I should meet him together with the Christians. I took two congregational presbyters with me. The Thikedar gave us a friendly welcome." During the conversation under the tree there appeared two Christians of the opposite side looking menacing and carrying sticks. Jellinghaus to them: "I asked them if they own the village and told them that I had come at the request of the Thikedars." This public recognition of the position of the Thikedars as the owner of the village opened the negotiations. "After half an hour they reached agreement and the Thikedar promised with a handshake that they should have their land and ordered that houses be built immediately and he gave to them the wood for that purpose."[156]

started to give sermons elsewhere (in a tent) at the same time of worship at Christ Church. They want to turn the members of the congregation of the Christ Church to their preaching." (Transl. U.S.).

156 Biene 1870, No. 5, p. 43 (Transl. U.S).

Jellinghaus's attitude in the conflict can be well understood given the Lutheran background. To accept the Thikadar in his secular role on the one hand in the discussion could have diplomatic reasons - to win him over. On the other hand the missionaries advocated the doctrine according to Martin Luther, who understood the secular authorities were appointed as a part of a divine order. In a general conference of the congregations in 1871 the missionaries and the native catechists, teachers and pastors discussed among other matters the question of land. A local teacher at the seminary, a certain Hanukh, presented the Lutheran view, which Jellinghaus implies and completes the discussion interestingly:

> "Listen brothers, so often you tell our beloved teachers and so often you complain about the Thikadars. But you are not right to do this, because very often you are suffering through your own fault and often lies are said to the Padri. Know, that the Thikadars are installed by God as persons in authority. They have received power over us; then we must also give what belongs to them. Now I know from contact and talking with you that most people hope to be freed from all authoritarian obligations by the adoption of Christianity. If that were so, then God would not have established such positions of authority. Dear brothers, I am sure, if we give the Thikadars what is right and proper, then we Christians will suffer much less than we are now."[157]

This Lutheran concept about authorities - here presented from a native - led to a reluctance of missionaries to be engaged in the land question. The Board/ Kuratorium of Gossner Mission in Berlin particularly supported this attitude. Chairman General Superintendent Carl Büchsel circulated in 1869 a pastoral letter to the congregations of the Indian mission field. It is a reaction to the specific situation of the division of the mission but also covers the social issues in the country. He wrote:

157 Biene 1871, No. 11, p. 84 (Transl. U.S.).

> "With cordial sympathy we have heard from the oppressions that you suffer from the pagan Zamindars. ... But Brothers, distance yourselves from violence, outrage, carnal self-help and all such things. God does not bless such methods and they just bring more misery and distress upon you. The Lord must help and He will do so. Pray that all may be fulfilled by the Gospel of Jesus Christ. If the Zamindars become Christians, all distress will end.... In your situation remember the word of St. Paul : 'Every person is to be in subjection to the governing authorities. For there is no authority except from God, and the existing authorities are established by God. Rom 13.'"[158]

Büchsel's attitude, which he had propagated also during the revolution in Berlin in 1848, is deeply rooted in Lutheran theology, as I have said. A change of external conditions cannot be brought about by violence. This was not only a learned lesson of the German Reformation, but there is also another aspect to it. The missionaries, through their analysis of the conversion motives of the Adivasi, felt confirmed in their Lutheran reluctance to become involved with land matters. They feared, that the conversion of the Adivasi to Christianity would remain superficial, if the land issue was their main interest. Very clearly Hermann Onasch verbalised this in an assessment of the mission field in 1870. He quotes an Adivasi question that he encountered again and again: "If the body does not survive, how can the faith survive?" Without any reported reply to that question, he describes the specific situation of Christians after the Sepoy revolt in 1858. After the revolution many Christians received generous payments as compensation by the British. Additionally presbyters went through the villages and promised that Christians would get back their lost land and be freed from compulsory labour.

> "The result were mass conversions to Christianity ... Our missionaries discover more and more how Christianity was initially adopted up by the Kols under the slogan: Sahai

158 Biene 1870, No. 5, p. 48 (Transl. U.S.).

> from the Sahebs; Freedom from the Thikadars; Recovery of all long lost possessions, if it must be, by perjury, opposition and revolution if it must be, also murder and manslaughter, and this all Prahbu ke nam se and Prabhu ki daya se (in the name of the Lord and the Lord's grace)."[159]

By distancing themselves from the land question the Missionaries wanted to avoid that the Christian faith would be adopted because of an expected external benefit. Their mission father Gossner had said: A Christian is one who has the call of Christ in his heart. The Missionaries remained faithful to that doctrine. One would misunderstand them and their theological reasons, if one would interpret this as an evasion. They were concerned about the spiritual existence of the mission. Addressing the land question would mean in their point of view an externalizing and thus endangering of the sustainability of the mission. The mission is saved only in the conversion of the inner man. Noticeable is their description of their reaction when they faced individual cases of the abuse of the Thikadars. Stereotype they say again and again: "We request them to pray". However, this did not mean that the problem should be dismissed. Instead, they want to establish through prayer a spiritual sympathy, compassion and closeness to the Adivasi on this extremely distressing issue. That's why after the division of the missionaries in 1868 the number of reports on the question of land to the German readers greatly increased seeking intercessions from abroad. Compared with other reports an inner sympathy can be seen here.

For example:

– Missionary Didlaukies tells about a visit in the village Changatola at Dumatoli where he encountered a Christian who is cheated out of his harvest every year by the Thikadar. He therefore does not have enough for his hungry children. Didlaukies: "It was a moment that I am unable to describe. But so great is the depth of the distress and bitter misery of some of our Kols-Christians. You have to wonder at how

159 Biene 1870, No. 3, p. 18 and 20 (Transl. U.S.).

firmly they still depend on their saviour ... One would almost be ashamed of one self. I tried to comfort them, urging them to persist in their prayers."[160]

- Hermann Ansorge tells of a visit to the village Palki, where he met a Christian who during his attendance at a service of worship in Ranchi was dispossessed by a "bad Thikadar called Manoram". He closes his report with the sigh: "May the Lord God look down soon on such misery!"[161]

As part of that inner sympathy, the missionaries start in the post-division period to learn the indigenous languages of the Munda and Oraon. This allows them to be much closer to the population and to pray with them. This inevitably leads now to the fact that distancing themselves from the conflicts on land issues becomes difficult. In the area of work of the missionary Didlaukies, two interesting cases are reported in which he locally overcomes the oppression of the Thikadars.

1) In 1870 in Hulsu, Didlaukies heard that the local Thikadar had not issued the receipts for payments already made and now he tried to increase the taxes. The Thikadar had caught the Christian landowners held them as prisoners on his terrace guarded by soldiers. Didlaukies went to the house and was also captured and bound by the soldiers and by the brother of the Thikadar. The landlord was not present at that moment. Didlaukies witnessed how a honourable old church member was beaten. In the late afternoon the Thikadar reached the place and saw with horror the bound Sahib. Didlaukies insisted on involving the police, which the Thikadar wanted to avoid. So, Didlaukies could negotiate fair deals for rural landowners with the Thikadar.[162]

2) In the spring of 1870 Didlaukies was fortunate to meet the manager of the Raja of Chotanagpur, whose responsibility it was to supervise the land property on behalf of the five-year-old son of the

160 Biene 1969, No. 2, p. 30 (Transl. U.S.).

161 Biene 1869, No. 12, p. 96.

162 Biene 1870, No. 2, p. 16.

deceased Raja. The supervisor, Mr. Smith, was apparently an English lawyer, and he was called Raja-Saheb. Didlaukies found in the Raja-Saheb Smith an understanding of the situation of Christians in the area of Gossnerpur/ Govindpur. So it was possible to instruct the local Thikadars to refrain from oppression.[163] For some years the situation was secure. Again, the Lutheran recognition of authority was a key to improving the local situation.

The second phase of the mission is therefore determined through the perception of the land question by the missionaries, by their Lutheran reluctance to act on the side of the Adivasi, by their spiritual guidance in prayer and from all of these, the initiative to mediate in local conflicts. Here, the missionaries were helped through Lutheran theology to accept Thikadars as authorities, which sometimes opened the door for negotiations.

The missionaries had found their own way to deal with the land question. At the same time, however, during this phase they left the German readers in ignorance about the other groups engaged in the Adavasi land issue.

c) Political distance – Sardare: socialist agitators

The single local solutions, which the missionaries found, aroused of course the impression that they could be more involved in the land question. This was the preserve of the so-called Sardars.

In 1889, the term Sardar was used the first time in the mission magazine of the Gossner Mission.[164] Sardars were local leaders - very often they were educated Christians - who collected funds in the villages to pay lawyers who fought for their land rights in court. However, the phenomenon occurred much earlier, namely around 1864 with the so-called "Kolkata-goers" as I have already mentioned. The Sardar movement had at the end of the 19th century a special dynamic. In 1887, a delegation of the Sardars joined the General

163 Biene 1870, No. 7, p. 62.

164 Biene 1898, No. 1, p. 6. Nottrott describes here the results of the petitition of the Sardars. He name them as "Sirdare" (sic) adding the explanation: The Sirdars are "the at the top of all malcontent standing leaders.

Conference of the missionaries, handing over a memorandum on the land question. It included 17 points, which Alfred Nottrott quoted in the more scientific General Missionary Magazine – "Allgemeine Missionszeitschrift". The demands of the Sardars included a restoration of an idealized primary status of land ownership of the Adivasi.

> "10th As our ancestors were free people, so we want it to be too. … 14th … Every nation rules in his own country, the English in England, the Chinese in China, the Germans in Germany - why should we the Mundaris and Uraus not be Lords in our country? … 17th … With the mission we have become wiser, we heartily thank you; But the Mission should help liberate us from our earthly distress."[165]

Nottrott saw clearly that the demands for an original Adivasi-kingdom could hardly be contested successfully in court. The Sardars still wanted the support of missionaries. As a result not only did the representatives of Munda and Oraon Sardars fall out with each other, but also the Sardars split away from the German mission. The last meeting of a deputation of Oraon Sardars with the missionaries contains a very interesting dialogue, which demonstrates once again the determination of the Lutheran missionaries, not to use worldly power.

> "'Do you want as German missionaries to help us rule the country or not?' Answer: 'No, we are missionaries and have no worldly power!' – 'Will you at least help us execute our program and be on our side?' - Answer: 'No, because it contains unreasonable and unfeasible demands.' – 'That's why we make the statement that from today all Uraus will leave the German mission.' Answer: 'You are free people and

165 Alfred Nottrott, Der gegenwärtige Stand der Kols-Mission mit besonderer Berücksichtigung der Landfrage, AMZ 16 (1889), pp. 270-271 (Transl. U.S.).

can do what you want, but know that you will answer for all that you do before God at the end of your days.'"[166]

Looking back Nottrott noticed that the missions feared a sizeable loss of Christians. But three years later, he mentioned that from 36.000 souls of the whole Adivasi Christian community only "1,295 souls apostatized or abandoned their faith".[167] In the following years until 1895 however the missionaries paid a lot of attention to the topic of the Sardars in their reports to the German readers. The Missionaries saw firstly the Sardar movement associated with the mission of the Jesuits. They wrote of the Jesuits sprinkling "poison".

> "What they allow to be preached, is the relief from the funds to be paid to the landlords, the lure of money and help of any kind; about Christianity more or less nothing is being said." The Jesuits would act in areas "where they could spread their poison without being disturbed by one of our catechists, but they disappear immediately if any one of us appears." [168]

Except to this single note it is remarkable that in the writings of the German Protestant missionaries we find only very few brief notes on the work of the Jesuit mission and on their attitude towards the land question. Apparently, there was little contact and debate between protestant and catholic missions in Chotanagpur. Nottrott complains symbolically about the "disappearance" of the Jesuit mission, when there was a risk of an encounter in the mission field. On the whole, it seems that the relationship of the missions in the 19th century in Chotanagpur would have to be researched using the different catholic and protestant sources.

Without any further reference to the Jesuit mission, Nottrott continues to report on the land question. So, in February 1892 he observed a local increase in the requirements of Thikadars as a result of the announcement of the Bengal Tenancy Act. In some villages

166 Ibid., p. 273 (Transl. U.S.).

167 Ibid., p. 278 (Transl. U.S.).

168 Biene 1989, No. 3, p. 23 (Transl. U.S.).

the Christians were innocently involved in several legal actions. The Thikardars did not issue receipts for paid taxes, so that they could make more demands and gather pledges.[169] Contrary to this, the Sardars tried to employ lawyers by raising money from the local people. They were successful in fundraising, because the need was great among the Adivasi. The missionaries admit this, but they have a special understanding and interpretation of it. Here are some examples:

– Missionary Püsching in February 1893: "Among the Christians in Tamar are socialist agitators, the Sardars, broke in and devastated a small congregation and they led 11 families back to paganism. On my way back ... I visited several villages outside Tamar, they are badly devastated by the Sardars. ... The poison of social democracy has damaged tremendously the Burju community. The number of souls which converted back to paganism through the Sardars is quite large and will continue to be quite significant in the coming years, because they always entice new groups away."[170]
– Alfred Nottrott in December 1893: "The main event of the month of September was a revival of the Sardar's deception. Already the waves had abated and for the Mundari communities, at least in Burju and Bandgaun, order began to return ... The new bait, which has been thrown out by the Sardars for trapping the masses, was their appointment of an English lawyer from Calcutta."[171]
– Again A. Nottrott in January 1895: "On my trip I heard in Tapkara to my delight, that the Sardar-movement was dying out there because the infamous Sardar Gideon told his parents in-laws, they should from now on go back to the church." The editorial added explanatory a footnote on

169 Biene 1892, No. 2, p. 9.

170 Biene 1893, No. 3, p. 28 (Transl. U.S.).

171 Biene 1893, No. 12, p. 91 (Transl. U.S.).

the Sardar-movement: "the socialist agitators in the Kol land issue." [172]

Apparently the Sardar-movement decreased for several years after 1895, they were quiet but had not quit. The probably continuation of the Sardar-movement may have been an essential background for the later success of Daud Birsa Munda.

It is noticeable in the reports of the missionaries that they compare the Sardar-movement with the social democratic movement in 19th century Germany. They describe the Sardars often as "sozialistische Wühler" - socialist agitators. What was the background to this?

The missionaries had observed how the social democratic movement in France and Britain had flooded into Germany. The term "socialist agitators" was often used in reports in the German newspaper. At almost exactly the same time as the term "socialism" is used in the letters of the missionaries describing the Sardars, the abolition of a law banning the social democracy was being vigorously discussed in Germany. After two assassination attempts on the German Emperor in 1878 the "Law against the public danger of Social Democratic endeavours" was adopted by the parliament. It forbade Social Democratic and Communist meetings. However, Parliament could not extend it beyond 1890. Therefore, conservative circles then feared a spread of social democratic ideas. At the same time, the Government of the Protestant Church in Germany (Evangelischer Oberkirchenrat) forbade its pastors in a circular letter the "direct participation of the pastors in social democratic gatherings, which are connected to speech and counter-speech....". [173]

This was the political background and the situation of the church when missionaries drew this comparison. They meant apparently: The objectives of the social democratic movement and the objectives of the Sardars are similar. The European Socialist wants a collective participation of the workers at the point of production

172 Biene 1895, No. 1, p. 2 (Transl. U.S.).

173 Heiko Oberman et al., Kirchen und Theologiegeschichte in Quellen, Bd. IV, Vom Konfessionalismus zur Moderne, Neukirchen-Vluyn 1997, p. 269f.

and collective participation in the profits. The dream of Sardars is an Adivasi-kingdom with equal land rights and also collective – socialist – participation in that. It seems that the Missionaries wanted to say by this comparison: Look, even in faraway India you have to have protection against the "poison of social democracy". Insofar as the missionaries reported extensively on these processes in the villages of the Adivasi, it contained a secondary political message for the homeland readers. However, the missionaries did not address in any of their letters to the German reader their detailed understanding of the relationship between Sardar-movement in India and socialism in Europe.

2.3 Summary

Primarily the missionaries reported only reluctantly about the land issue to Germany during the first phase. With their division in 1868 the reports and their comments about the land issue increased due to the activities of the counter-mission. They found in this second phase an effective spiritual way of dealing with the land question. Since this apparently created disappointment, and further oppression of Thikadars arose, the Sardar-movement increased in its importance. In this third phase the Missionaries remain consistent in their Lutheran attitude and in their distance to the Sardars. In addition, there probably was a secondary political motive to distance themselves from the Sardar-Movement. That was wise. Because, a connection between the German Mission and the political movement of the Sardars would probably have meant in the upcoming conflict about Birsa Munda the end of the German Mission in Chotanagpur.

3. Birsa Munda and Thomas Muentzer – Evangelical and Social freedom[174]

The history of the Lutheran churches starts in Germany. Associated with this history is the social movement of the peasant war. From a conflict between Martin Luther and the peasant movement a number of theological principles evolved, which distinguished the evangelical approach from that of the social freedom movement.

The history of the Lutheran church of Chotanagpur starts with the arrival of the missionaries. Likewise and in a similar historical setting as that of the peasant war, an uprising of the rural population took place.

Looking at the individual historical situations as well as the personalities of Thomas Muentzer and Birsa Munda, a comparison of the two seems very worthwhile. It points towards a parallel contextualisation and towards the question: What is the relation between evangelical freedom and social freedom, what is the relation between the preaching of the Gospel and the social revolution?

It seems impossible to present all the available material. I will, therefore, just briefly talk about the history of Thomas Muentzer (1). Then I will share with you my understanding of Birsa Munda (2) which I have mainly derived from letters of the missionaries. This I will do more comprehensively in the hope that some of these details

174 Lecture was held on 3rd November 2011.

will also be new for you. Finally, I will try to compare the two (3) and finish with some conclusions (4).

3.1 Thomas Muentzer[175]

Muentzer was born in 1489 in Stolberg (Harz). He studied theology at the University of Frankfurt/Oder and was ordained as priest in 1513 in the diocese of Halberstadt. Between 1517 and 1519 he was frequently in Wittenberg where he came into contact with Martin Luther. He preached in Jueterbog as a reformed cleric. Luther himself recommended him to the Saxon city of Zwickau where the population was receptive to the concept of reformation. However, after a short time, problems arose in Zwickau Muentzer had radical reforms in mind. The exact circumstances of the conflict are no longer easy to determine. Finally, he was expelled from the city in 1521. His last receipt slip he signed with the words: "Thomas Muentzer, who fights for truth in the world."

From Zwickau he went on to the city of Prague in Bohemia. One of his most important publications from this period is still in existence, the Prague Manifesto. In this paper, Muentzer lays out in detail a strongly apocalyptic point of view. He wrote that the final days had started, the time of harvest, and that God was sending his prophets, and that Muentzer himself was one of them. The people of Prague, however, assessed the situation differently and expelled him from Bohemia. He now turned to Allstedt where he found employment as a preacher. It was during this period that he worked on the reform of the liturgy, the main point of this being the introduction of the German language into the holy mass. For this purpose he translated Gregorian hymns into German. It was due to this act that Luther saw himself forced to reform the mass. On July 13th, 1524, Muentzer held his so called "Sermon to the Princes"[176]

175 Siegfried Bräuer/ Hans-Jürgen Görtz, Art. Thomas Müntzer, in, Martin Greschat, Gestalten der Kirchengeschichte, Vol. 5, pp. 335-352. Hans-Jürgen Goertz H.-J., J. Jaquiery & P. Matheson, Thomas Müntzer apocalyptic mystic and revolutionary, Edinburgh 1993.

176 The full text is available: http://http-server.carleton.ca/~jopp/3850/6-1.htm.

at Allstedt in front of Duke John and his son John Frederic. In this sermon he urged the Dukes to act diligently according to their responsibilities since the final period leading to the judgement day had commenced. In August 1524, however, he had to escape from the authorities in Allstedt and go to Muehlhausen. From there he continued to South Germany where he met peasant farmers who were in revolt. He joined them because he realised that this was the time of judgement, indeed the time of the final battle had arrived. The peasant riots mobilised large sections of the population. About 60.000 peasants rose up in Thuringia. The details of this uprising cannot be discussed here. The battles came to an end on May 15th, 1525, when 8.000 peasants were confronted with a much smaller army of the Saxon-Hessian leaders. The farmers lost. Muentzer was sentenced to death. During the court case, he claimed that the riots had failed because of the selfishness of the rioters.

3.2 Birsa Munda

The life and work of Birsa Munda cannot be wholly understood without considering the preceding Sardar movement. However, this cannot be addressed here.[177] Instead, it might be of special interest, when portraying Birsa Munda, to listen to the perceptions of the missionaries. They were the first ones to write reports about him. Of course, it has to be kept in mind that they conceived him as a "false prophet", "false Christ" and the like. Due to these judgments, we can nowadays only have a fragmented impression of this person.

When visiting the mission sites in 1894, the mission inspector Karl Heinrich Christian Plath identified from the church registers the date of birth of Daud Birsa Munda as 22nd July 1872.[178] In the year of

177 Cf the paper "Social movement of the Adivasi during the 19th century in Chotanagpur reflected in German Sources" in this book.

178 Karl Christian Heinrich Plath, Gossners Segensspuren in Nordindien. Eine geschichtliche und missionstheoretische Beschreibung, Friedenau 1896, p. 79. "In the register of Burju I saw, that Birsa Munda was a Christian. He was baptized throgh the missionary Kröcher, born on 22nd July 1872, baptized at 11th August d. J., together with his parents."

this visit, the missionary Karl Puesching, who was resident in Burju, described Birsa Munda and the fledgling movement for the first time in a letter. He wrote that Birsa Munda was just nineteen to twenty years old.[179] He had visited the mission school in Chaibassa when his parents removed him from the school because they had turned away from Christianity. During his school career he had certainly learned some of the basics of the Christian faith. They appear as separate aspects in his own doctrine. He faced his "calling experience" as a result of a stroke of lightning or thunderbolt. He was roaming in a forest with friends searching for a treasure which had been revealed to him in a dream[180]:

> "As they were working, out of the blue, a bolt of lightning struck the ground in the midst of them all; nobody was injured, but Daud was transformed in such a way that his skin was no longer dark but whitish." According to Puesching, Birsa Munda explained this to his parents this way: "I have received evidence from heaven that I am not your son but the "son of man", sent by God and ordained as father and redeemer of the world. You and all mankind must serve and worship me."[181]

As a sort of short version of the "doctrine" of Birsa Munda, Karl Puesching states the following:

179 Following this, he was born 1875/76. Biene, February 1896, p. 10: "Six month ago a false prophet arose, Daud is his name. He is a young man about 19-20 years old. With the lie of the Sardar-Movement his parents fell back to the pagans. When they were Christians their son visited our school in Chaibasa." (Transl. U.S.).

180 Helmut Borutta tells not about a treasure hunt but about necrophilia, which brought Birsa Munda out of the village community. Borutta has taken his version of the legend from Suresh Singh. But, Puesching's report is the older source. Suresh Singh, The dust storm, p. 39. Helmut Borutta, Revolution für das Recht, p. 21.

181 Biene 1896, February, p. 10 (Transl. U.S.).

> "His doctrine was as follows: 'I am the son of God, sent from heaven and ordained as God and father by the heaven. You have to believe in me. If you trust in me, I assure you that I will support you, if you do not believe in me, I will destroy you. … Working on Sunday is not a sin, but Monday is a resting day. You may dance and drink as much as you like. You shall never give a sacrifice, neither when you are sick, nor when you are working in the field, or in any other case. You may not wear shoes. … I do not oppose the Christian religion, it is good. The Sahibs (Europeans) have preached the Gospel correctly, but they have corrupted the original religion by approaching the altar in shoes or boots and wearing them elsewhere although the shoes are made from the skin of cattle. The Lord Jesus never used boots or a sun hat. Moreover, the padris and catechists have distorted the Christian religion by collecting money during the service, by charging fees for special acts, by banning jewellery, by handing out the Holy Communion. How can you eat your redeemer! It is not correct that the padres hand over the corpse of Jesus for consumption.'"[182]

According to the education Birsa Munda had, we find a number of elements of various religions in his doctrine. The refusal to wear boots in front of the altar, for example, and the exclusion of cattle skin may have been adopted from Hinduism. This includes the rule set up by Birsa Munda and reported by Puesching elsewhere to wear a Brahman string and to eat vegetarian food only.[183] Besides these attributes, which may well indicate a Hindu influence but not

182 Ibid., p. 10 (Transl. U.S.).

183 Biene 1897, August, p. 58: "When the false Messiah was kept in prison under his disciples come up a kind of doctrine. In a special catechism, in that way they call this book, they collect all what this cheat said. When the Christians go to the Sunday service to the church the scholars of Birsa Munda sitting under shadowing trees and make church. … Their Catechism teaches that everybody should wear a string similar to the Brahmans, and that they should not eat meat! " (Transl. U.S.)

a Hindu origin[184], Christian thoughts obviously dominated Birsa Munda's syncretism.[185] Birsa Munda appears to be the one, who cleans the Gospel from all those supplements, which in his view had spoilt it. This includes the practice of preaching by the European missionaries, the collecting of money and the concept behind the Holy Communion. Birsa Munda apparently opposed this by creating his own preaching practices. Puesching for example reports that his disciples celebrated specific services following a specific catechism.[186] It appears that social issues played a more central role than in the services of the missionaries. In this issue, the objectives of Birsa Munda were quite close to those of the Sardar movement.[187] The goal of the Sardars and that of Birsa Munda were the same: to build up an empire of the Adivasi which would put a stop to land expropriation.[188] In addition to this social dimension within Birsa Munda's perception, two more religious motives must be added. They consist of his consciousness of his divine mission and, on the other hand, of an apocalyptic vision:

- Divine mission: The consciousness of his divine mission, as described previously, corresponded with the belief of his disciples. The fact that the discipleship of Birsa Munda grew

184 For a hinduistic background we miss some elements like the Varna-system. Birsa was against this. Franklin Baxla, Birsa and Freedom Struggle, p. 49.

185 Victoria Luker, Millenarism in India. The Movement of Birsa Munda, in: Geoffrey A. Oddie, Religious Traditions in South Asia, Interaction and Change, Richmond 1998, pp. 51-64. Luker means without knowing the sources of the missionaries elements of the syncretism of Birsa Munda are based in the myth of the Mundas and the Hindus.

186 Cf. note 183.

187 Biene 1900, June, p. 41f. "It is clear that the Sardar-Movement and the Birsa-movement unify themselves. The heads didn't confess this officially. But it is known that Sardar Gideon 1895 had secret meetings with Birsa. ... That the riot today is a Sardar-riot confess the former catechist Yakub in the prison of Chaibassa with the words: "*Chinaing Chikaya jhandhanagentele laraikena*" – we had struggled for the banner of rights." (Transl. U.S.).

188 Biene 1900, p. 41. "The aim of Birsa and of the Sardars was to build up an empire, that's why he was called "ote Abba" father of the earth."

so rapidly was, in view of the missionaries, the result of a certain naivety of the indigenous population.[189] They were said to be manipulated by reports of miraculous healings and a resurrection of Birsa Munda from the dead, behind which Puesching – and this is not unlikely – presumed very "earthly" reasons.[190]

– Apocalyptic vision: Birsa Munda saw that a comprehensive "revolution" or "upheaval" of everything that existed would take place in a short space of time. Hence, he proclaimed that fire would rain down and that the earth would quake. In this case he advised his disciples to stop all field work and the care of livestock.[191] This apocalyptic perception gained a very special importance since it matched the religious traditions of the Munda as well as those of the Hindu. Both religions anticipated a Golden Age. In the case of the Munda, this is even to be initiated by the incarnation of the creator God Singbonga in a child.[192]

A violent riot led by Birsa Munda was the unavoidable consequence of the combination of the consciousness of a divine calling, the apocalyptic vision and the goal of social liberation. His disciples had gathered in a village called Chalkad. The police,

---

189 Biene 1897, August, p. 59.

190 Biene 1896, February, p. 11. Puesching comments the story of the resurrection of Birsa Munda: "The truth was, the new abba of the earth had an attack of diarrhoea. But nobody should know this ... His own sister, she is today still a Christian in a village nearby told me this secret." (Transl. U.S.)

191 Biene 1896, February, p. 11. Püsching tells: "After some days he ordered his followers: "Go from village to village and tell everybody who wants to be rescued, to come to Abba on 27th of July at 12 o'clock. At the same day we have to face an earthquake and fire will fall from sky. But, who stays beside the Abba will be rescued. Cry into the world: It is not necessary to seed, to ploughing, planting, slaughter and eat all chicken, goats and sheep..."" (Transl. U.S.).

192 Justus M. van der Kroef, Patterns of Cultural Change in three primitive Societies, in: Social Research Vol. 24. No. 4 (1957), p. 431. About the concept of Munda religion: Marsallan Bage, Phänomenologie der Munda-Religion, Berlin 1960.

however, was there before the rioters. After the first attempt to arrest Birsa Munda had failed, the police took him by surprise in the night from 31st August 1895, while he was asleep. Although he cried out, nobody came to help him. The reports by Puesching and Singh are consistent on this point.[193] The day after, Birsa Munda was transferred to the city of Khunti. There he was sentenced to three years in jail following a court case. However, this did not terminate the movement.

The movement continued among the indigenous population. Missionary Kiefel reported in August 1898 that the "Birsa nightmare" might arise again, "if a leader were to be found, we would certainly experience something here". [194] Still the Sardar disciples tried to promote the issue of land title deeds. The extent to which the "doctrine" of Birsa Munda still affected them, even three years after his arrest, can be seen in a footnote of Kiefel saying that "the Sardar disciples believe the empire was theirs".[195] Mission Principal Alfred Nottrott in his annual report from June 1899 counts "two thousand members of this social-religious sect".[196] The inner circle would roam around "with their swords drawn".[197] Even mission stations and churches became the targets of these attacks because the Birsaits now accused the Christians of destroying the old Adivasi culture. When Birsa Munda was finally released from jail in 1900, an uprising was initiated which ended at mount *Sail Rakab*. Birsa Munda escaped. The British bribed four indigenous people, who then betrayed the leader by revealing his hiding place and that of his two wives. Whilst the soldiers kept themselves hidden, the four indigenous people convinced Birsa Munda to lay down his weapons by pretending to be some of his disciples: "Immediately Birsa was tied. He did not defend

193 Biene 1896, April, p. 28. Singh: The Dust Storm and the Hanging Mist, pp. 59-61.

194 Biene 1898, August, p. 59.

195 Ibid., p. 59.

196 Biene 1899, June, p. 43.

197 Ibid., p. 43.

himself, but his wives tried very hard to do so. They quietened down only after receiving some heavy punishment."[198]

In June Nottrott writes to Berlin that during his services in jail he had tried to approach Birsa Munda. He was also present at one of the main court sessions.[199] Finally, he reports that Birsa Munda died of cholera on June 9th and that his corps had been burned on the banks of the river.[200] From various comments made by the missionaries it can be seen that they presumed that the riot movement had not yet come to an end. However, later on the missionaries succeeded in launching a law, which is still in effect nowadays and which secures the land ownership of the indigenous population, the "Chota Nagpur Tenancy Act".

3.3 A Comparison: Birsa Munda – Thomas Muentzer

3.3.1 Historical Social Situation

Birsa Munda and Thomas Muentzer, both appeared on the stage of world history in social environments, which are easily comparable. The conflict between differing legal systems, the rise of taxes and the land grabbing characterised the rural setting of Chotanagpur in the 19th century.

But let us start with Germany: Although, there were great variations in the situation in differing regions of Germany in the 16th century, we can still generalise that it was the competition between various legal traditions as well as the rise of taxes and prices in the

198 Biene 1899, June, p. 22f. In Suresh Singhs book we found different versions of the arrest. But all versions are common that a betrayal was behind. Suresh Singh, The Dust Storm, Notes & References Chapter XII, p. 34.

199 Biene 1900, August, p. 61: "To see Birsa again I went to the court case and I sat two steppes beside him. When he saw me he closed his eyes and didn't look up to me." (Transl. U.S.).

200 Ibid., p. 61: "He himself was taken to another court; he passed away on 9th of the same month from cholera. His corps was burned in the presence of the jailor." (Transl. U.S.).

peasant economies, which resulted in the revolts in the rural areas.[201] Up to this time it was part of the village autonomy ("Dorfehrbarkeit") to settle legal cases at their own level; however, from his point on a feudal landlord appeared from outside to represent the interests of the government. Particularly in the North-Eastern part of Germany, the prosperous landlords exercised authority on land and other legal issues. Taxation, restrictions on free settling, on inheritance rules and on the utilisation of communal forests, etc., resulted in a deterioration of the living standards of the local people and a revival of serfdom.

Let us take a look at Chotanagpur now: Here, we find the indigenous Khuntkattidar system. The Khuntkattidar was the one who cleared the land and who remained the owner of that land even if it was cultivated by other families. In the 17th century, however, a king appeared who claimed to have the right of taxation over that land. He installed tax officers, the Zamindars and the Jagirdars. When taking over the sovereignty of Chotanagpur in 1771, the British authorised the Zamindars to act as the official police force thus leaving the indigenous population virtually without any rights.[202]

When comparing the situation in Germany of the 16th century and Chotanagpur of the 19th century, we realise a conflict of differing legal systems to be the cause of impoverishment and social deprivation. In Germany we find the legal system of the village, the village autonomy. This system is comparable to the Khuntkattidar system. Later, the landlords have the right of taxation over the land and they themselves are subordinate to a king – thus they have to pass on taxes – in this, they are comparable to the Zamindars. In Chotanagpur of the 19th century as well as in the states and territories of the German Empire of the 16th century, these social conditions resulted in unrest and riots. This was a long time before Thomas Muentzer and Birsa Munda appeared. In Chotanagpur we find the uprising of 1831/32, which was put down by the colonial power, the Sardar movement and the rebellion of Birsa Munda. As for the German Empire we

201 Heinz Schilling, Aufbruch und Krise, Deutschland 1517-1648, 4. Ed. Berlin 1998, pp. 140-144.

202 Hellmut Borutta, Revolution für das Recht, p. 47.

have the uprising of the peasants in the movements of the south (Bundschuh) and finally the emergence of Thomas Muentzer.

3.3.2 The Persons of Muentzer and Munda

A description of the doctrine and the fate of Birsa Munda could be derived in part from the reports of the missionaries. The main issues were a) the prophetic consciousness of his mission, b) his apocalyptic vision and c) the intention of social liberation by means of rebellion. On all these three levels we can find parallels to Thomas Muentzer.

a) The consciousness of a mission

First of all, Birsa Munda and Thomas Muentzer are similar in their pretension to follow and implement God's will more clearly than the rest of the world due to their exclusive relationship to God. Thomas Muentzer, though not identifying himself as the son of God as Birsa Munda did, at least referred to himself as the servant of God. Differing from Luther, who used the same term, Muentzer used this title in a much more apocalyptic and prophetic sense.[203] This can be illustrated by the change of self-designations in his correspondence. In a letter from 1521, he calls himself "Thomas Muentzer, servus electorum dei" (servant of the people from God elected), "Thomas Muntzer, a servant of God against the Godless"[204] or "Thomas Muntzer with the sword of Gideon".[205] What forms the background of his prophetic mission is mainly rooted in his spirituality. He saw

203 Luther used the title "servus dei" bzw. "servus christi" in his letters to Spalatin. Cf. WA Br. 1, 44,1 (16); 50,1 (27); 77,1 (30). Cf. Gerhard Ebeling, Lutherstudien Vol. 3, Tübingen 1985, p. 10 f. ; p. 11 note 21.

204 For all quotes of Muentzer I use the German critical edition: Thomas Müntzer: Schriften und Briefe, ed. By Günther Frantz, Gütersloh 1968 (abbr. Müntzer, Complete works), p. 456, 6. But there is also an English edition available: Thomas Müntzer. Pater Matheson. ed. The Collected Works of Thomas Müntzer. The important text of the "Sermon on the Prince" can be found: http://http-server.carleton.ca/~jopp/3850/6-1.htm.

205 Müntzer, Complete works, p. 470,15.

himself as having understood the Christian faith in a more profound way than others.[206] In a letter he explains this experience:

> "For the faith the size of a mustard seed must throw the huge mountain of our selfish love into the sea of all our ambitions. Then Christ, who is the true son of God, will join those, who drown therein and find no comfort. Christ will join them in the night, when misery is at its highest. The chosen ones will believe that he is the devil, or that he is a ghost. But he will say: 'O ye beloved ones; do not be afraid, it is me, I cannot enlighten you in any other way. There is no other way to pour my grace into you.'" [207]

In this freely fabricated quotation of Christ, the way of dedication to the Gospel of faith appears to be exclusive. There is no other possible way to experience faith or come to faith because Christ "cannot enlighten ... in any other way". Muentzer at this point reproduces his own experience, and it is likely that the core of the exclusive understanding of his mission consciousness lies here. It is because he encountered Christ on the night of his deepest misery through the same type of suffering, that he concludes that this is the only way to encounter Christ. Muentzer, in his own view is the one person, more than any other, who understands the fundamentals of faith.

Now comparing the mission consciousness of Birsa Munda and Thomas Muentzer, we first find a topical difference between the two. According to the witness of Puesching, Birsa Munda called himself "son of man", the "father and redeemer sent and ordained

206 Ibid., p. 495,11-13. "Ich sage auff mein allerhöchstes pfandt, das ich meinen mercklichsten und allerhochsten fleyß furgewandt habe, das ich muchte vor andrn menschen hochlicher erkennen, wie der heilige, unuberwindliche christenglaube gegrundet weher." I say according to my highest pledge, I give my best effort, that I will understand better that other people, how is the holy unconquerable Christian faith founded. (Transl. U.S.).

207 Ibid., p. 425, 3-13 (Transl. U.S.).

by God".[208] It is reported several times that his disciples called him "Abba". All these titles are from the point of view of the Christian tradition definitely divine designations. However, in the concept of Birsa Munda, they did obviously not conflict with Christian perceptions of God, which in fact he accepted as described earlier. Thomas Muentzer on the other hand strictly keeps this distinction between God and man in his consciousness of mission. He labels himself as servant, but not as redeemer.

Nevertheless, the titles of Birsa Munda as well as those of Thomas Muentzer are meant to describe their special message, their special relationship to God placing them in a special, exclusive role as opposed to others. In the same way we will also have to interpret the issue of the calling experience. Whilst Puesching reports on the thunderstorm experience of Birsa Munda as his very particular impetus for his mission, no such event has been testified in the case of Muentzer. For Birsa Munda, this incident became the basis for his exclusive mission. As for Thomas Muentzer, this initiating function of a calling experience can be found in the exclusive experience of his faith, which is basically founded as faith in the "abyss". This is the basis of his exclusive mission. Although being different in the religious foundations of their particular mission consciousnesses, the messages as related to their respective person are quite similar: the fate of the world depends on them alone. Birsa Munda: "You have to believe in me. If you trust in me, I assure you that I will support you, if you do not believe in me, I will destroy you."[209] Thomas Muentzer: "The time of harvest has arrived! Therefore, God himself has sent me into his harvest. I have sharpened my sickle."[210]

b) Apocalyptic expectations

It was during his time as a preacher of Reformation in the Saxon city of Zwickau where the apocalyptic-prophetic identity of Muentzer became public. Luther was the one who had sent him there in 1520.

208 Biene 1896, February, p. 10.

209 Ibid., p. 10.

210 Müntzer, Complete works, p. 504,18-24 (Transl. U.S.).

It is not very clear which circumstances caused this transformation. After all, in the Prague Manifesto composed after his dismissal by the council of the city of Zwickau, the apocalyptic momentum of his theology is clearly elaborated. It states that the church had lost the innocence of the apostolic age "due to those academics", who "always want to sit on top". They have neglected the election of the priests by the congregation and during their councils they have only dealt with "childish games".[211] It is time now that "the chosen friends should also learn God's word".[212] In his sermon of 13th July 1542, Muentzer used this apocalyptic notion, by which the kingdom of God was just ahead and the time of assembling had come. This was the "Sermon to the Princes" about Dan 2, which he preached at the castle of Allstedt in front of Duke John, his son John Frederic and other representatives of the Saxon government.[213] Obviously identifying himself with the prophet Daniel, he awarded the sovereigns a crucial role in assembling the church of the chosen. It would be their duty to destroy the Godless with their sword. However, if they failed to do so, the Christians would have the right to oppose their sovereigns.[214] Since this was, in the view of Muentzer, already the case, he consequently said:

> "It can clearly be seen that the Dukes do not respect the Christian faith at all. Hence, their power is also coming to end; it will be handed over to the ordinary people in a very short time."[215]

---

211 This summary of the apostasy of the church can be found in all versions of the Prague Manifesto. Müntzer took them from his reading of the apostolic fathers Hegesipp and Eusebius. According to this the church was a pure virgin up to the last Bishop of the apostolic age. Müntzer's Complete works, pp. 493, 31-494, 8.

212 Ibid., p. 494, 10-12.

213 http://http-server.carleton.ca/~jopp/3850/6-1.htm.

214 Ibid., p. 328, 27-329, 9.

215 This summary of the apostasy of the church can be found in all versions of the Prague Manifesto. Müntzer took them from his reading of the apostolic fathers Hegesipp and Eusebius. According to this the church was a pure virgin up to

This attitude, targeting the renewal of the original church for the chosen in the final days, ultimately led to the battle of Frankenhausen.

The closest structural convergence between Thomas Muentzer and Birsa Munda can be seen in the apocalyptic expectation and its immediate effect. Two aspects can be directly compared:

Renewal: Thomas Muentzer's starting point was the renewal of a pure church, purified from all the mud of false teachers and authorities. Very much alike and as described earlier, Birsa Munda was of the opinion that the doctrine of Christ had been perfect but was corrupted by the Sahibs (the Europeans). The concept of a genuine religion is combined with the social question of the Sardar movement. The coming kingdom is the kingdom of the renewed original land ownership. Thomas Muentzer as well as Birsa Munda conceive a pure status of originally unspoilt conditions, which would be realised in the near future due to an apocalyptic revolution.

Final battle: Muentzer believed that the renewal of the kingdom of the chosen would be established soon after the last rebellion of the antichrist. It was crucial to find the right attitude towards this message spread by Muentzer. Any form of government has to be therefore subordinate to the kingdom, which immediate arriving was expected. This resulted in the battle of Frankenhausen. On the other hand and parallel to this, Birsa Munda announces the proximity of a coming kingdom on several occasions. And likewise, the future fate of the people depends on their attitude towards him and his message. He announces the immediate end of the current situation and the beginning of a new empire with the old laws re-established. Therefore, the fields no longer need to be cultivated, tax-paying is no longer necessary and obedience must no longer be shown to the existing authorities. This led to the battle at Sail Rakab.

---

the last Bishop of the apostolic age. Müntzer's Complete works, p. 417, 23-25, (Transl U.S.).

c) Opposition to the sovereign – social freedom

As already described, Muentzer first pronounced the responsibility of the sovereign to use his secular power to establish the new church of the chosen. However, Muentzer's expectations were disappointed. In addition to the measures taken against him personally, he notices social conditions, which demonstrate that the sovereign is in fact a constraining factor for the church of the chosen. The true faith cannot fill the hearts of the people since the ordinary people are mainly occupied by securing their livelihoods. The poor are kept away from reading and the sovereign is proclaimed as being ordained by God[216], whilst in fact the sovereign "takes a bath in the soup of exploiting, stealing and robbing" in such a way that "all creatures on earth … the fish in the water, the birds in the air, the yield of the land are all theirs".[217]

The stimulus to develop a "theology of resistance" came from outside the church. The peasant riots which spread from the south-west of Germany to Thuringia were identified by Muentzer as apocalyptic indications. Now, it was the Lord himself leading the fight against the sovereigns, who did not fulfil their welfare duties.

The social need, denounced by Muentzer, that the birds and the fish in the water and the yield of the land belonged to the sovereigns, is similar to the conditions of the peasants of Chotanagpur in the 19th century. It is almost with the same words that the consequences of tax increases imposed by the Zamindars are described. Besides this obvious topical parallelism it is also true for both Thomas Muentzer and Birsa Munda, that an already existing social movement and a religious apocalyptic figure meet one another. In the beginning, Birsa Munda, according to the witnesses of the missionaries, still pursued religious objectives. Only after his first arrest and release

216 This summary of the apostasy of the church can be found in all versions of the Prague Manifesto. Müntzer took them from his reading of the apostolic fathers Hegesipp and Eusebius. According to this the church was a pure virgin up to the last Bishop of the apostolic age. Müntzer's Complete works, p. 275, 26-38.

217 Ibid., p. 329,15-21.

we find a closer association with the socially motivated movement of the Sardars. Similar with Thomas Muentzer, active resistance only started after the peasant movement had spilled over to Thuringia and his recognition that this was an indication that the final days had begun.

3.4 Evangelical and social freedom

Although Birsa Munda and Thomas Muentzer appeared in different ages and areas of world history, in a review the similarities are quite evident. The socio-historical background to their actions was characterised by the conflict of differing legal systems. Both were convinced of their prophetic pretensions, claiming that the further course of world history depended on the attitude of people towards themselves and their environment. Both saw an empire arising, where existing injustice would be abolished and lost religious and social rules would be re-established. Finally, they identified the violent rebellion of great numbers of oppressed peasants against the ruling sovereigns as an indication that the final days had arrived. With their prophetic pretensions, they placed themselves at the peak of a battle – and failed.

Their fate has written into the collective memory of the Christian church the everlasting task to clarify the relation between the freedom of the Gospel and social liberation. The attitude of the missionaries towards this dilemma was determined by political (1) and theological (2) motives.

1) Politically, the missionaries rejected Birsa Munda and the Sardar movement because their activities were dependent on the colonial administration. The more the riots spread, the more reports were sent to Berlin, which reflected their indignation: rumours publicly accused them of influencing and partly causing the riots. From their point of view it was obvious that they had to defend themselves against such allegations so that the accusations would not jeopardise their presence. Although, they were trying to distance themselves from this movement, the mission inspector Karl Heinrich Christian Plath clearly identified that the movement had Christian

origins. During a visit in 1895, he had the opportunity to talk to Birsa Munda and in his review he writes: "It seems just impossible that this whole affair would have developed into such a complete and acute danger if there were no Christian ideas behind it."[218] Yet he added, the movement was motivated by a false interpretation of the Gospel.

2) Theologically, Plath like all his fellow missionaries had studied Luther's catechism, which they carried in their luggage when embarking for Chotanagpur (CA 16 and 28). Here, we find the so-called "doctrine of the two kingdoms" or "the two reigns of God". It states that God rules in a twofold way, a spiritual and a secular. The spiritual reign shall lead to faith through preaching and the sacraments. The secular one shall take care of the external order within a society. In a social revolutionary movement, however, these two powers are combined into one. This leads to the situation that the spiritual power takes over the duties of the secular one too. By doing so, it contradicts the peaceful message of the Gospel by threatening to use and by actually using violence. Finally, the spiritual power contradicts its basic objective to lead people towards freedom of their conscience through the justification of faith if this is forced by external jurisdiction or revolutionary violence. Freedom of faith would then no longer be an issue of a free conscience, but that of a law masked as a social rule.

Even though the immediate parallelisation of spiritual and social freedom can be solved theologically, still two questions prevail that seek answers in the respective contexts:

- How can the doctrine of the two kingdoms be true if the sovereign is not maintaining the social order and, therefore, obviously not from God? The missionaries were not prepared for a transfer of Luther's doctrine of the two kingdoms into non-christian context.
- How can a church actively comply with the Gospel of the Nazarene and actively advocate for the captives, the blind

218 Karl Heinrich Christian Plath, Gossners Segensspuren, p. 79.

and the bruised (Lk. 4:18) without damaging the individual freedom of conscience and without anticipating the impact of the grace of God?

The conflicts, in which around Birsa Munda and Thomas Muentzer were involved, have written these questions into the memory of the worldwide church. Let us keep our ecumenical dialogue on these issues alive.

Section 4

Ecumenical Approaches

1. The Jubilee Centenary of Edinburgh 1910-2010 and its heritage today

In year 2010 the Ecumenical Movement celebrated the hundredth anniversary of the World Missionary Conference in Edinburgh.[219] Up to now, the assessments of this conference have been very diverse. Some associate this conference with a spirit of mission dominated by the west, a spirit considered as having been overcome by the modern conceptions of "partnership in mission" or "contextualisation." Others perceive the conference's burning will to evangelise the world as a continuous ideal. Again, others remember Edinburgh 1910 as a historical date marking the beginning of the Ecumenical Movement. Such different assessments pose the question: is there a heritage of the World Missionary Conference for us nowadays, and if there is, what is it, and what does it mean for our partnership? We will deal with this question in two steps: (1) the history and (2) the limitations and chances for us today, resulting from the Conference.

1.1 History

It had long been observed that the dispersion of the Protestant mission did not support the worldwide spreading of the Gospel. The dispersion began with the time of the Awakening in the nineteenth century, when most mission societies were founded as free conventions. Often they saw themselves in opposition to established churches. Their vision

219 The Lecture was held on 1st October, 2009.

not only consisted of the spreading of the Gospel but likewise aimed at awakening Christians in the traditional churches through news about conversions in distant countries.[220] The name of the mission journal issued by J. E. Gossner, may serve as an illustration. He called it "The Honey Bee on the Mission Field." He conceived this title as a picture: the honey bee flies to far away countries, and the best she collects is the pagan honey serving to awaken the dead and sleepy Christians of Germany.[221] The assumption borne by this picture, that the mission would help to awaken the local church, reveals the spirit of the age of awakening that most societies felt committed to.

This general intention of the smaller mission societies to awaken the Christian churches in old Europe consequently resulted in the need to keep some distance from institutional and organisational matters. The motivation to contribute to the awakening of the church called for an attitude of critics and critical distance from the church. The task was to transform the church into a living congregation of Christians by heart. This transformation, however, could only come from an outside spirit. This was the reason why many smaller or larger mission societies grew at a distance from the church. They pursued their own missions and tried what the traditional churches hardly achieved: they established networks through their mode of sending personnel and they established networks in the countries in which they operated. National mission conferences were launched, among others in India. In the context of these national corporations, a need for an international cooperation of churches in mission became apparent. Finally, on 14-23 June 1910, about 1,350 official delegates convened in Edinburgh. They mainly originated from Anglo-Saxon

---

220 Rebekka Habermas, Mission im 19. Jahrhundert-Globale Netze des Religiösen, in: Historische Zeitschrift 187 (2008), pp. 629-679. Rebekka Habermas/ Richard Hölzl, Mission Global, Köln 2014.

221 Biene, 1834, No. 1, p. 1: "Her honey (scil. of the Bee) is all the time beautiful and delicious. And the best is: It is Heather-Honey ... serving for the healthiness of the pagans as well as for their awakening, enlightening and reviving for the sleepy Christians, who approach the pagans." In German the word "Heide" (Heather) has a similar sound for the word "Heide" (Pagans). The preface of Gossner was also published in the first edition after his death No. 4 in 1858.

and European mission societies. Among them were delegates from the relatively small Gossner Mission[222] as well as a minor group of 19 delegates from the young churches of those days. Those mainly came from Asia, with eight from India.[223] Alongside the Conference, an extensive auxiliary programme was offered, attended by up to 6,000 visitors, daily. The World Missionary Conference may well be claimed as having been the largest Christian assembly to date.

The participants enthusiastically experienced a previously unknown unity of churches. An eyewitness noted that "The world has never seen an assembly like that of Edinburgh. I would say, the diversity was surprising, but even more surprising was the unity."[224] The reports often talk about the "unanimity or unity of the spirit." This consisted of the common goal to win the world for Christ. This unanimity is demonstrated in great self-confidence in the concluding "Message from the Conference to the Church," which states that in the spirit of mission, a degree of unity had been experienced that had never been achieved among the churches up to then:

> "...and in this endeavour we have reached a greater unity of common action than has been attained in the Christian Church for centuries."[225]

It was due to the fact that this experience of unity was missing in the local churches at home that the Conference gained such importance. This atmosphere was fostered by still another aspect. The missionary "kairos" was felt to be present: now is the time of mission.

---

222 World Missionary Conference 1910, Vol. 1-8, London/Toronto, 1910, Vol. 9, The History and Records of the Conference, together with Addresses Delivered at the evening meetings, Edinburgh/London 1910, p. 66. Among the Participants are named: Missionary Pf. Hertzberg, Sup. Dr. Matthes, Rev. P. Richter and Rev. Vogel.

223 Brain Stanley, The World Missionary Conference Edinburgh 1910, Studies in the History of Christian Missions, Grand Rapids, 2009, p. 50f. and p. 90f.

224 A. W. Schreiber (Hg.), Die Edinburger Welt-Missions-Konferenz, Basel 1910, p. 20.

225 World Missionary Conference 1910, Vol. 9, p. 108.

The enthusiastic mood towards the opportunities of mission was supported by the worldwide dominance of Protestant empires and the invention of new technologies (aviation, telegraphs, railways). It seemed likely that the whole world could be Christianised in the near future. Hence, the concluding Message states:

> "The next ten years will in all probability constitute a turning point in human history, and may be of more critical importance in determining the spiritual evolution of mankind than many centuries of ordinary experience. If those years are wasted, havoc may be wrought that centuries are not able to repair. On the other hand, if they are rightly used, they may be among the most glorious in Christian history."[226]

In reviewing the Conference, a German mission scientist pointed out that, "It is the atmosphere of 'Yes, we can!' that characterises the Conference and keeps it moving."[227] The spirit of mission, however, is not just one that identifies the opportunity of open doors; more precisely, one would have to speak of a spirit that urges one into mission. The concluding Message of the Conference clearly emphasises that the right time of mission is now, only now.

The main objective of the meeting was to analyse the practice and the conditions of the recent missionary activities and to gain a new impetus for the mission out of this exercise. Therefore, a two-year evaluation process was carried out in preparation for the Conference, covering eight topics and involving 600 missionary experts from overseas and home. This exercise resulted in eight introductory volumes which later on served the delegates as preparatory materials, and which may be considered as excellent sources of missionary history.[228] These reports were introduced during the Conference and

226 Ibid., p. 108.

227 Wolfgang Günther, Edinburgh 1910 – gemeinsam die Welt für Christus gewinnen, in: Mission Erfüllt? Edinburgh 1910 – 100 Jahre Weltmission, Jahrbuch Mission, 2009, p. 18.

228 World Missionary Conference 1910, Vol. 1-8, London/Toronto, 1910.

discussed under strict limitations of time for oral contributions. Of course, it is impossible to list those results in detail. However, the most important issues may be specified:

1. The first day was entitled "Carrying the Gospel to All the Non-Christian World." It tried to gain an overview of the coverage of Christianity in all known parts of the world. The discussion revealed that a global expansion of Christianity would be a tremendous task, which could only be achieved by a common plan and better co-ordination of the traditional churches. In this context, special emphasis is laid on the "superhuman factor" of mission. It is God himself providing the power of mission and opening doors for preaching the Gospel.[229]
2. The second working group and the second day of the Conference dealt with the topic, "The Church in the Mission Field." Mission could only succeed if the churches themselves took up their roles as carriers of mission to the non-Christian world. The young churches in particular were to be motivated in their missionary efforts. The vision was that the missionary would only serve as an assistant in a church that was being newly established.[230] This was incorporated

229 World Missionary Conference 1910, Vol. 1, p. 352: "Everything vital to the success of the movement to carry the Gospel to all non-Christian world depends upon the power of God Himself. In His hands is the Government of the world.... His providence has opened the approach to the non-Christian countries..."

230 World Missionary Conference 1910, Vol. 2, p. 267f: "The relation in which the Church life in the mission field should stand in each case to the life and government of the parent Church; involving, on one hand, the recognition of the autonomy and liberties of the Church in the Mission Field; and, on the other hand, the maintenance of such mutual affect and respect between the young Church in the mission fields and the older Church in the west, as shall enable the latter to continue to give to the former helpful and sympathetic guidance when needful, lest in natural eagerness of young life growingly conscious of its own powers and capacities, and simulated by racial and national aspirations, it

into the concluding Message from the Conference to the churches in the non-Christian world:

"It is you alone who can ultimately finish this work: the word that under God convinces your own people must be your word.... But we rejoice to be fellow-helpers with you in the work...."[231]

3. The following day, the report of the third working group was discussed: "Education in Relation to the Christianisation of National Life." It is here where the numerous schools founded by missionaries were being reviewed. They were seen as instruments to disseminate Christian ideals and ideas beyond the church walls.
4. The fourth working group dealt with "The Missionary Message in Relation to Non-Christian Religions." Of course, Christianity was perceived as the absolute religion as opposed to a widely "decaying" paganism. The only way of meeting this absoluteness of Christianity would be to make it absolute by conquering the world.[232] The Conference tried to find a compromise between a radical rejection of other religions on the one hand, and the notion that Christianity was the most eminent religion, fulfilling all aspirations of other religions.[233] In a practical sense, the second perspective

---

should be led by inexperience and immaturity to break off hastily from old ties, and so multiply the divisions of Christendom."

231 World Missionary Conference 1910, Vol. 9, p. 110.

232 A. W. Schreiber, Die Edinburger Welt-Missions-Konferenz, p. 124. "Die Botschaft der Mission ... fordert uns auf unsere Überzeugung von der Absolutheit des Christentums dadurch zu bekennen, dass wir es wirklich absolut machen, in dem wir die Welt dafür erobern." The message of the mission requires that we our persuasion of absoluteness of Christendom recognise when we make Christianity absolutely in occupation of the world. (Transl. U.S.).

233 World Missionary Conference 1910, Vol. 4, p. 279. In the summary are two attitudes obvious. At the one hand they follow the path of the Church father Tertullian, who recognise in other religions the work of Satan. At the other hand they follow the more including path of the Church father Origenes,

is given clear priority. Other religions should not be met with hostility but should be directed towards a higher level:

"But nothing is more remarkable than the agreement that the true method is that of knowledge and charity, that the missionary should seek for the nobler elements in the non-Christian religions and use them as steps to higher things ... and that in their higher forms they plainly manifest the working of the Spirit of God. On all hands the merely iconoclastic attitude is condemned as radically unwise and unjust."[234]

This implies that this superiority is combined with the concept of a Christian religion modifying itself in contact with other religions. A German visitor to the Conference noted that the full wealth of the Gospel would only unfold once they had contributed their "experience and uniqueness." We will "discover new aspects within our own Gospel, see new light which we never saw before." We will have to come back to this issue later.[235]

5. On day five, the Conference discussed the topic of "The Preparation of Missionaries." During the preparation phase, missionaries complained about a lack of special education to meet the challenges faced abroad. The discussion on that day, however, did not really tackle the question of better training and focused instead on the belief of the missionaries and how to deepen their faith as a moving force.
6. The sixth working group conferred on "The Home Base of Missions." The objective here was not only to discuss how mission work could be financed by public relation activities and how mission societies could be supported. The most important aspect was the spiritual awakening of

who shows that the noblest of the old religions is fulfilled in Christ. Both understandings are caused by the New Testament and no contradiction.

234 Ibid., p. 267.

235 Ibid., p. 124.

the traditional churches for the task of the mission. These churches themselves would have to make the mission their own task. The perspective of an integration of church and mission comes into sight in the concluding "Message from the Conference to the church":

"We need supremely a deeper sense of responsibility to Almighty God for the great trust which He has committed to us as members of this conference. That trust is not committed in any peculiar way to our missionaries, or to societies, or to us as members of this Conference. It is committed to all and each within the Christian family and it is as incumbent on every member of the Church."[236]

To engage this trust in the mission would result in the faith of the churches being strengthened. If mission is happening and visible, the Gospel itself will reveal its power: "The strongest evidences of the power of the Gospel are to be found in the mission field."[237]

7. The seventh day of the Conference was dedicated to "Missions and Governments." This mainly included topics of practical relevance, such as work permits for missionaries or the quest for governmental support in banning the trade of opium and alcohol.
8. The topic of day eight touches the heart of the Conference: "Cooperation and the Promotion of Unity." The source of this spirit of unity as described by the common task of mission, is Christ. In his Valedictory Address, Sir Andrew Fraser (a friend of the late Ferdinand Hahn) notes:

   "We should not care for it half so much if we did not realise that it was the Lord Jesus Christ in our meetings that produced this spirit of unity. We have not felt this unity, not because we have wanted to feel it ... but because we have

236 World Missionary Conference 1910, Vol. 9, p. 109.

237 Ibid., Vol. 6, p. 266.

gathered round the one realising the one work that He has given to all to do."[238]

Having completed this overview of the various partial results of the World Missionary Conference, we now want to turn to the questions: what remained afterwards, what are the enduring tasks, and what has become obsolete?

1.2 Limitations and Chances

Only a few years after the Conference, the First World War began. This entailed a further dispersion of the Protestant missions and hindered the mission's path to unity. The national aspect was combined with the confessional one of the mission. This can easily be demonstrated through the example of the GELC and its path to independence. The German Lutheran missionaries were expelled from India during the First World War as a consequence of the sinking of the passenger ship "Lusitania" by the German forces, a cruel war crime with women and children as victims. After the expulsion of the missionaries, the mission in Chotanagpur was put under the auspices of the Anglican bishop, Dr. Westscott. At first, he guaranteed the preservation of Lutheran confession. Later on, however, he sought a union between the Lutheran congregations of the Adivasi and the Anglican ones.[239] This was only the way to gain independence and self-ownership of the church that finally secured the Lutheran confession. Accordingly, what was the spirit of unity in the mission, emphasised in Edinburgh as more important than any confessional boundaries, worth, if the Anglican church strived to simply incorporate the German Lutheran mission? Only the declaration of independence of the GELC secured the original state of confession and finally the acceptance of other churches. The synergy of politics and confessional issues was more important than the determination to co-operate on a common goal, God's mission.

238 World Missionary Conference 1910, Vol. 9, p. 343.

239 Hans Lokies, Die Gossner-Kirche in Indien, durch Wachstumskrisen zur Mündigkeit, p. 61f.

Apart from this temporal failure in the course of the First World War to achieve the high objectives of the World Missionary Conference, we can identify long-term outcomes. First of all, I want to outline the structural consequences, followed by an analysis of the substantial heritage, which are worth addressing.

a) Structural consequences

- National Christian Councils were established in countries in order to co-ordinate the various actors in their missionary efforts. Up to now, these Councils are politically significant representatives of the Christians in their countries across confessional boundaries.
- The International Missionary Council in Geneva was founded to observe worldwide missionary efforts and to promote mutual contacts.
- Finally, the series of World Missionary Conferences initiated in Edinburgh became one source of the later Ecumenical Movement (unification of the WCC and IMC in New Delhi, in 1961).

b) The Substantial heritage

Looking at the individual results of the Conference, we can already identify a number of issues characterising a modern missionary theology. For example, the later *Missio Dei* Theology is already there in the finishing statement of Fraser, quoted earlier on, calling Jesus the true actor of the mission.

As for our partnerships today, two aspects seem significant to me: our attitude towards other religions and the question of the unity of the mission regarding a view of the traditional churches.

Our attitude towards the others:

The fathers of the World Missionary Conference in Edinburgh were children of their time. This becomes obvious in the fourth section, "The Missionary Message in Relation to Non-Christian Religions." In fact, it was assumed that the end of other religions was in sight. In this context, the aim would be to enforce the preaching of the Gospel as a better religion. A colonial perception of one's own religion becomes apparent. However, and unlike some contemporary assessments suppose, the Conference chose a concept of esteeming other religions, thus allowing contacts in respect.[240] Any intolerance, state the minutes of the Conference, any "iconoclastic attitude is condemned as radically unwise and unjust" (Cf. Point 4).

Unlike the atmosphere that the Conference supposed, it has become obvious that Christianity is not the only religion but will be one religion among others for quite some time. In fact, this concurs with the spirit of the Gospel: we as Christians are the salt of the earth (Mt. 5). Keeping this reality in mind, the question arises as to how to deal with other religions. In the Ecumenical Movement, a "Code of Conduct" is being discussed, which in my opinion will only be realistic if the idea of mutual respect will be likewise accepted by those other religions.[241]

Even more interesting for us today is the fact that the fathers of Edinburgh did not cease in assuming the superiority of the Christian faith. They were convinced that through its contact with other religions and cultures, new aspects of the Gospel itself would come to the surface. This particularly included interpretations of the Gospel as evoked by contact with other religions and myths unknown to the western world. Such new interpretations may deepen the faith, since they illustrate the full wealth of the Gospel. The concluding Message of the Conference even urges such unfamiliar experiences of renewal with the Gospel:

240 Dieter Becker, Den Anderen mit Achtung und Ehrerbietung zugewandt, in: Mission Erfüllt? Edinburgh 1910 – 100 Jahre Weltmission, Jahrbuch Mission 2009, p. 85.

241 This Code of conduct was published after the lecture as a joint declaration of the Roman Caatholic Church, the World Evangelical Alliance and the World Council of Churches: Christian Witness in a multi-religious world. http://www.oikoumene.org/en/resources/documents/wcc-programmes/interreligious-dialogue-and-cooperation/christian-identity-in-pluralistic-societies/christian-witness-in-a-multi-religious-world?set_language=en.

> "Assuredly, then, we are called to make new discoveries of the grace and power of God, for ourselves, for the Church, and for the world; and, in strength of that firmer and bolder faith in Him, to face the new age and the new task with a new consecration."[242]

This is even more intensified by the previously mentioned call of the Conference for the young churches to find their own words to express their faith. It almost seems as if the fathers foresaw the need for an indigenous theology. "The word that under God convinces your own people must be your word,"[243] is written in the Final Statement. It is certainly in accordance with the spirit of the Conference when the GELC – as I notice it – develops steps towards an Adivasi theology in a contextual Bible interpretation and places special emphasis on the social dimension.[244] We can be quite grateful for this, as well as for the tradition of the inter-religious Prayer Day within the GELC, in which the church is far ahead in comparison to its churches of origin.

The attempt of contextualising may only then be problematic, once the contextualisation is set as equivalent to the Gospel itself, so that the specific contextual interpretation is no longer seen as a transformation of the Gospel among other transformations of the same Gospel. Ignoring the difference between the one word Gospel and contextual interpretation transformation makes the idea of a worldwide unity of the mission, impossible.[245]

---

242 World Missionary Conference 1910, Vol. 9., p. 109.

243 Ibid., p. 110.

244 Christ Sumit Abhay Kerketta, Adivasi Theology, Towards a Relevant Christian Theology for the Jharkhand Adivasi, Ranchi 2009. Jhakmak Neeraj Ekka, Taking to the Efforts of Reinterpretation of the Gospel and Creation of Literature in the Face of the Challenges we have today, in: Ulrich Schoentube, Zwischen Wort und Tat, Beiträge zum 150. Todestag von Johannes Evangelista Gossner, Erlangen 2009, pp. 48-63. Anand Sebeyan Hemrom, The Needs for Ecumenical Efforts in Mission Activism in the Face of Threats to Adivasi Identity, Survival Existence, in ibid., pp. 64-79.

245 Cf. the preface of the book.

The unity of mission:

The vision of the unity of the worldwide mission is the main heritage of Edinburgh. It is very much worth considering what it means for us today to be part of God's mission and to be part of a worldwide co-operative. It means that we follow God's mission, the *missio Dei*. We guide each others' views towards the different cultural images (not just one image) of the Gospel, and we enjoy this. Furthermore, this entails that within God's mission, we are united as equal partners. From this, however, we have to formulate one critical comment and one step ahead, from the Edinburgh fathers.

The critique: In Edinburgh, the unity of the mission was primarily conceived as a unity of the missionary spirit of the acting western Mission societies and only a few young churches. Although recognised, these churches were addressed separately. It was commonly agreed that missionary assistance from the west was needed to avoid the self-destruction of the young churches during conflicts.

The step ahead: Nowadays, we may characterise the unity of mission in equal rights as a mission to six continents. Once we identify the heritage of Edinburgh as the unity of mission and accept our equal rights within the *Missio Dei*, then we will have to say: The old western churches do not have anything in prevalence to the young churches. To have equal rights in the unity of the mission means to be on the way, together, like the Emmaus disciples. They need one another in order to guide one another to the Gospel.

Finally, we will have to critically examine ourselves: how near or far is our relation to the ideal of a partnership in mission in equal rights, and to what extent do we realise the spirit of the worldwide unity of the mission? Traditionally, does the Gossner Mission support the mission efforts of the GELC, and vice versa? It is time, now, 100 years after Edinburgh, to be serious in our efforts towards the worldwide unity of the mission in terms of equal rights: ask the German visitors about their missionary life! Ask when you visit Germany. Search for it and show interest in the mission in Germany! We need you as brothers and sisters of Emmaus.

2. Tolerance and Mission

In the previous sessions we have discussed[246] in terms of the Birsa Munda movement the social relevance of the Gospel. From here the question arose whether a special enculturation of the Gospel could be recognised in the expression of a social movement. Thus, we studied the report on the first conversion and discovered that in the mission the missionaries themselves became learners. In the meal communion leading to conversion[247], they learned that the message of the equality among sisters and brothers was the prime motive to become Christians.

If we understand mission as a community of learners, the question should then follow: how such learning processes work and what the preconditions are. What is the relation between the truth claim of our own faith and the faith and religion of others? What does tolerance mean in the mission, how far does it reach and where are its limits?

In order to enter into a discussion, I would like to take you on a three-step path: The perception of tolerance in the Bible, the old church and in reformation; Concepts of tolerance; Dialogic tolerance in the latest mission declarations of the World Council of Churches.

---

246 The lecture was held on 19th January 2013.

247 See the article in this book: "Mission as Misunderstanding – Observation in Conversion Processes".

2.1 Tolerance in the Bible, Old Church and Reformation

a) New Testament and ancient world

Christianity developed in a religious landscape. The dispute with other religious doctrines was there from the onset of the Christian faith. This can be appeared very well in the parable of "the weeds in the wheat" (Mt. 13) in the New Testament. The final judgment on the true doctrine of a person's own or any other religion is being transferred into Day of Judgement. The coming Son of Man will judge, not the church. Thus, the judgment is being withdrawn from man, and man can do no more than just grow as "good wheat" together with the weeds, tolerating the weeds.

This text in the New Testament has repeatedly been discussed in Christian literature since the maturing Christian Church, in its contact with other religions, had to balance itself again and again between two principles, which originated in the time before Christianity became a state religion in Rome.

1) In the ancient world of the Roman Empire, it was a rule, particularly in critical times that the welfare of the empire and the state depended on the right worship of the gods.[248] Religion was an instrument to stabilise the authority – similar to national-Hindu concepts aiming at matching the area of a religion with that of the state. This resulted in the widespread systematic persecution of Christians in the ancient world. One principle, therefore, is the

248 Cassio Dio, Roman History LII, 36, 1-2: "Therefore, if you desire to become in very truth immortal, act as I advise; and, furthermore, do you not only yourself worship the divine Power everywhere and in every way in accordance with the traditions of our fathers, but compel (ἀνάγκαζε) all others to honour it. Those who attempt to distort our religion with strange rites you should abhor and punish, not merely for the sake of the gods (since if a man despises these he will not pay honour to any other being), but because such men, by bringing in new divinities in place of the old, persuade many to adopt foreign practices, from which spring up conspiracies, factions, and cabals, which are far from profitable to a monarchy. Do not, therefore, permit anybody to be an atheist or a sorcerer." (http://penelope.uchicago.edu/Thayer/E/Roman/Texts/Cassius_Dio/52*.html)

intolerance towards other religions in order not to jeopardise the coherence of the state or the community.

2) The other principle, pertaining mainly in peaceful times, was to integrate other religions. This was based on an inclusive perception: behind different religions and religious concepts, one paramount power would be concealed.[249] Hence, no one can be forced into a specific religion.

When Christianity first became a tolerated religion under Constantine and the state religion later, in the year AD 380, by an edict of Emperor Theodosius I, Christianity adapted these two principles of tolerance and intolerance with their specific motives. On the one hand, the theologians repeatedly emphasise the freedom of faith. For instance the church father, Augustinus, states that one only believes in one's heart, which cannot be compelled.[250] The great medieval theologian, Abaelard, unfolded, in a fictional dialogue between a Jew and a Christian, the picture that behind religions, in their historical appearance, there is a universal level of one reason.[251]

On the other hand, a principle of intolerance established itself and the association of the young Christian religion with the power of the state was an important prerequisite for this. The religious truth claim, the observance of which assured the nature of the state, could

---

249 Quintus Aurelius Symmachus, III Relatio 10: "It is right that we that, what all worship, see as one ultimate reality (quidquid omnes colunt, unum putari). At the same stars we look up, the sky we all have in common, the same universe encompasses us. What does it matter in which doctrine one seeks the truth? On a single path one cannot reach such the high mystery." (Transl. U.S.) (http://www.hs-augsburg.de/~Harsch/Chronologia/Lspost04/Symmachus/sym_re03.html)

250 Augustin, Tractatus in Iohannis Euangelium, 26,2. "A man can come to Church unwillingly, can approach the altar unwillingly, partake of the sacrament unwillingly: but he cannot believe unless he is willing. If we believed with the body, men might be made to believe against their will. But believing is not a thing done with the body. Hear the apostle: "With the heart man believeth unto righteousness." And what follows? "And with the mouth confession is made unto salvation." That confession springs from the root of the heart." (http://www.ccel.org/ccel/schaff/npnf107.iii.xxvii.html)

251 Peter Abaelard, Dialogus inter Philosophum Judaeum et Christianum (1140).

be enforced with power. This can easily be demonstrated in the edict Cunctos populos from AD 380, whereby Christianity is being promoted into the Roman state religion:

> "It is our desire that all the various nations which are subject to our clemency and moderation, should continue to profess that religion which was delivered to the Romans by the divine apostle Peter, ... According to the apostolic teaching and the doctrine of the Gospel, let us believe in the one deity of the father, the son and the holy spirit, in equal majesty and in a holy trinity. We authorise the followers of this law to assume the title of catholic Christians; but as for the others, since, in our judgment they are foolish madmen, we decree that they shall be branded with the ignominious name of heretics, and shall not presume to give to their conventicles the name of churches. They will suffer in the first place the chastisement of the divine condemnation and in the second the punishment of our authority which in accordance with the will of heaven we shall decide to inflict."[252]

Nothing can be found here any more of the patience advised by the parable of the weeds among the wheat, whereby the coming Lord will judge. The judgment on the other religions and Christian denominations, the "foolish madmen", shall be executed by the power of state well in advance. The unity in religious issues should guarantee the welfare of the state. As a result of the acceptance of the Christian faith as state religion, the question of the truth of doctrines became, at the same time, a question of the truth of the existence of the state. This is why heretics were persecuted rigorously.

---

252 Theodosius I. Edikt "Cunctos Populos" (Edict of Thessalonica) in: Codex Theodosianus, XVI, 1.2. Clyde Pharr, Theresa Sherrer Davidson, The Theodosian code: a translation, with annotation, of all source material of Roman Law, Nashwille 1945. English text also at: https://en.wikipedia.org/wiki/Edict_of_Thessalonica.

In this sense, the association of state and church in the ancient world was a significant precondition for the expression of an intolerant attitude towards other religions and religious concepts within Christianity. In the course of history, however, even the other principle was wondrously conserved: the perception that faith cannot be forced.

b) Reformation and the consequences

Due to the Reformation, a new chapter in the issue of tolerance was opened in the history of Christianity. There was now a need to find new ways of cohabitation between groups calling each other heretics. The starting point for this new development was Luther's appeal to the individual conscience.

In the beginning of the history of the Reformation, Luther stood in front of the Diet of Worms. All electors were assembled in front of the emperor hearing the case and the criticisms Luther had formulated against the Pope on the issue of justification. When Luther was summoned to revoke, he said:

> "Unless I am convinced by the testimony of the scriptures or by clear reason … I am bound by the scriptures I have quoted and my conscience is captive to the word of God. I cannot and will not revoke anything, since it is neither safe nor right to go against conscience. May God help me. Amen."[253]

It is true that Luther explains his refusal to revoke primarily with the argument that the authority of the Bible is superior to the doctrines of the church and above the Pope. Yet, this prioritisation of the scriptures is actually a free decision of conscience.[254] When Luther was held in protective custody in Wartburg castle translating the Bible, there were violent riots in the city of Wittenberg. People

253 Deutsche Reichsakten, Jüngere Reihe Bd. 2, Gotha 1899, reprint Göttingen 1962, p. 803,4-8 (Transl. U.S.).

254 Martin Brecht, Martin Luther, Vol. 1 Sein Weg zur Reformation 1483-1521, Stuttgart 3rd ed. 1990, p. 439.

abolished the rituals of the Catholic mass and removed paintings and altars from the churches. The leader of the riots, Andreas Bodenstein von Karlstadt, argued exactly like Luther did, claiming that he followed the Holy Scriptures with his conscience. It would also be authoritative with its ban on images. Luther, being called back to Wittenberg, replied in his well-known Invocavit sermons, that he respects the appeal to the conscience, yet he warns: You do not change the conscience and the heart of the believers by external reforms but solely by preaching and the Holy Spirit. God himself executes the task of the Reformation and the revival of faith through his word:

> "I do not have the hearts of the people in my hands like a potter has his clay to do with them what I like to do (Rom.9:21). I cannot reach any further than to their ears. I cannot reach into their hearts. Since I cannot pour the faith into the hearts, neither can nor shall I force or pressurise anybody, because it is God alone who does it and makes that is already alive in the heart beforehand. [255] ... I have only taught, preached and written God's word. I have not done any other thing. It was this word that has done so much in weakening the papacy while I was sleeping and drinking Wittenberg beer with my Philipp and Amsdorf."[256]

---

255 WA 10/3 p. 15c 4-12. "dann jch hab nit in meiner gewalt oder handt jr hertzen (der menschen) als der haeffner den leymen, mit jm zuschaffen nach meynem gefallen. Ich kan nit weytter kommen dann zů den orn, jns hertz kan ich nit kommen: dieweyl ich dann den glauben jns hertz nit giessen kann, so kann noch sol ich niemants darzů zwingen noch dringen, wenn got thut das alleyne und macht, das er vor jm hertzen lebt. Darumb sol mann das wort frey lassen und nit unser werck darzu thůn: wir haben wol jus verbi aber nicht executionem. Das wort soll wir predigen, aber die volge sol got alleyn in seim gefallen sein." (Transl. U.S.).

256 WA 10/3, p. 18.13-19.3: "ich bin dem ablas und allen papisten entgegen gewesen, aber mit keyner gewalt, jch hab allein gottes wort getrieben, geprediget und geschrieben, sonst hab ich nichts gethan. Das hat, wenn ich geschlafen han, wenn ich wittenbergisch bier mit meynem Philipo und Amßdorff getruncken hab, also vil gethan, das das Bapstum also schwach worden ist, das jm noch nye

Relaxed and free, this is how the Invocavit sermons sound. And one is inclined to read later and modern categories of freedom of conscience out of them. However, Luther justifies this freedom theologically, writing that nobody may be forced into anything in issues of faith. Faith is given by God. Hence, no one may anticipate God, but one can only reach unto the ear with words. The sereneness to drink "Wittenberg beer", however, has limits for the Reformators. The inner side of man is free in issues of faith and so it is subordinate directly to God. The external side of man, however, is living in a setting, set by the same God who has liberated the conscience or the heart. Whoever threatens this setting or order acts against God. Now, the subjectivism of faith and conscience propagated by Luther resulted in the fact that a whole wing of the reformation movement took this right of appealing to the conscience, thus challenging the structures of the state, for granted. Luther noticed the danger that man would rise up against God's order. Actually, we can recognise this as a similar, though modified, expression of the ancient principle described earlier: the correct performance of religion helps in stabilising the structures of the state; it cannot overthrow the structure of the state. Attacks against the governing authority as propagated by Thomas Muentzer – in trying, like Birsa Munda, to implement an equal distribution of goods – were sharply condemned by Luther. He recommends to the sovereigns to defeat the uprising of the peasants. In doing so and opposing his own appeal to the conscience and the resulting freedom, he denies that the peasants' appeal to conscience and scriptures was justified.

> "The rulers, then, should press on and take action in this matter with a good conscience as long as their hearts still beat. It is to the rulers' advantage that the peasants have a bad conscience and an unjust cause and that any peasant who is killed is lost in body and soul and is eternally the devil's. … Therefore, dear lords, here is a place where you

---

keyn Fürst noch Keyser so vil abgebrochen hat. Ich hab nichts gethan, das wort hatt es alles gehandelt und außgericht." (Transl. U.S.).

can release, rescue, help. Have mercy on these poor people! Let whoever stab, smite, slay. If you die in doing it, good for you! A more blessed death can never be yours, for you die while obeying the divine word and commandment in Romans 13:1-4."[257]

Hence, we find both principles with Luther: the tolerance and freedom of conscience – this concerns mainly the inner side of man in front of God – and the intolerance, in that a doctrine and its expression would be equally disputable in the social structures of the external side of man. In these violent conflicts, the Reformation movement became guilty by acting against dissenters. This was even known by Luther as we know from his scriptures on the peasant war.

In preparation for the Reformation jubilee year 2017, the Evangelical Church in Germany specifically considers the subject of tolerance. In 2012 a critical dispute is being held with more emphasis on the "shadows" of the Reformation than of its achievements. This evaluation is as far as I am concerned difficult, because historical criteria are being used, which were not there at that time. The Lutheran concept of freedom of conscience developed into the modern concept of a legally binding freedom of religion only centuries later. This was first done by the settlers in America in the "Virginia Declaration of Rights" of 1776, which legally implemented freedom of religion and opinion and the separation of the governing authority and the church. In Prussia, the seemingly tolerant country of origin of the Gossner missionaries, there was a more liberal policy

257 Martin Luther, Wider die stürmenden Bauern, WA 18, p. 360, 12-15.24-28: "So soll nu die oberkeit hie getrost fort dringen und mit gutem gewissen dreyn schlahen, weyl sie eyne ader regen kan, Denn hie ist das vorteyl, das die bawren boese gewissen und unrechte sachen haben, und wilcher bawr darueber erschlagen wird, mit leyb und seele verluren und ewig des teuffels ist....Drumb, lieben herren, loset hie, rettet hie, helfft hie, Erbarmet euch der armen leute, Steche, schlahe, wůrge hie, wer da kan, bleybstu drůber tod, wol dyr, seliglichern tod kanstu nymer mehr uberkomen, Denn du stirbst ynn gehorsam goettlichs worts und befelhs Ro. am 13. und ym dienst der liebe, deynen nehisten zurretten aus der hellen und teuffels banden." (Transl. U.S.).

of settlement by the king. It may be recalled that Johannes Gossner served in a congregation of Bohemian refugees, the Bethlehem church. Calls for the free choice of religion, however, changing the denomination and converting, only arose in the 19th century, with the establishment of the free churches of the Baptists, Mennonites, etc., who, for themselves, claimed a freedom of confession which should even be extended to all religions. It was only in 1919, when the separation of church and state was put into effect – it was there, in varying shapes, since the ancient world – that freedom of religion became part of the constitution. A liberal and tolerant attitude of the state in issues of religious affairs of various confessions and religions only became possible when the embrace of state and religion was broken.

c) Pragmatic and dialogic tolerance

At that time, when the connection of state and religion was dissolved, the freedom of conscience announced by Luther resulted in a pragmatic tolerance of the state. The state abstained from enforcing its own religious truth claim for the benefit of a valued esteemed higher purpose: peaceful communion and the welfare of society. This tolerance is a highly valued asset though not respected by everybody, as the 21st century shows. What happens if a religious group, which does not accept the philosophy of neutrality of the state and the freedom of conscience, stands up, as is the case in fundamentalist groups? Never mind whether these groups are Christian, Hindu or Muslim, they seem to grow constantly, although the freedom of conscience is fixed in more and more constitutions. The paradox coming up now is: The state must possibly ensure tolerance and the freedom of conscience by using legal and even intolerant measures. It is, if you wish, the intolerance of the tolerant against the intolerant.

We have our problems with this paradox of the philosophical neutrality of the state that one may have to protect the values of peace by using violence, which is contradictory to peace. The sceptical view is even increased once the freedom of conscience is not constituted theologically in relation to God like it was with Luther, but constitutes a value of man himself. However, where do people and society receive these values from? It was right in the 20th century when democracies bore dictatorships, who now furnished their self-made values with a religious character as can be seen in the German Nazi ideology and in Soviet communism.

In this paradox of tolerance of the liberal democracies that appears nowadays, mainly in our interaction with fundamentalist movements and parties, the question of how much strength the religions can mobilise to support a peaceful cohabitation becomes vital. In my view, there are some promising approaches towards an extended definition of tolerance in the Christian faith. The pragmatic tolerance described so far orients itself on the secular frame of states and is in line with the original sense of the word. The Latin word, "tolerare", means "to endure patiently". In other words: the tolerance of a state means that it patiently endures various basic religious orientations of its citizens and their respective reasons for their conscience binding, as long as the general principle of a peaceful coexistence is not threatened.

Now, an active role, in terms of tolerance, could crop up from the religions. This would mean not just patiently enduring the religious orientation of others but making them acceptable, in an active sense. What is needed is a dialogic tolerance, which actively approaches people with other faith, seeks conversation and lets itself become involved in a common search for the truth. This can be justified within the Christian faith by the fact that grace and mercy, even the fullness of life is there for all mankind. However, how can such a dialogue be implemented by a religion, which is determined by mission? Starting points can obviously be found in the latest mission declarations of the World Council of Churches (WCC), which shall now finally be presented.

2.2 Mission declarations

a) Code of Conduct

In the year 2011, the WCC, the Catholic Pontifical Council for Inter-Religious Dialogue and the World Evangelical Alliance – hence the majority of global Christianity – agreed upon a Code of Conduct, called "Christian Witness in a Multi-Religious World".

The declaration in its first section focuses on the "basis for Christian witness". Two aspects are mainly elaborated on. On the one hand, it emphasises that it is part of the nature of Christian faith to give witness of Christ. This witness, however, is not done by the Christian alone, but he is part of the mission of God into the world. In conjunction with the Gospel of John, it is said that the believers are assigned to witness to the world as the father assigned the son.[258] It is appealing to discover that a mission statement of Johannes Gossner appears here, he also having said that the Christian was sent into the world like the father sent the son, thus enabling Gossner to conclude, smilingly: those who have not been sent by Christ "shall stay at home".[259]

The other aspect of the missionary foundation of this declaration is the freedom of conscience and faith, which had formerly been newly discovered by Luther. Following this, a conversion to Christian faith cannot be enforced: "Conversion is ultimately the work of the Holy Spirit (cf. John 16:7-9; Acts 10:44-47). They recognize that

258 http://www.oikoumene.org/resources/documents/wcc-programmes/interreligious-dialogue-and-cooperation/christian-identity-in-pluralistic-societies/christian-witness-in-a-multi-religious-world.html. "Jesus Christ is the supreme witness (cf. John 18:37). Christian witness is always a sharing in his witness, which takes the form of proclamation of the kingdom, service to neighbour and the total gift of self even if that act of giving leads to the cross. Just as the Father sent the Son in the power of the Holy Spirit, so believers are sent in mission to witness in word and action to the love of the triune God."

259 Johannes Evangelista Gossner, Missionspredigt, in: Johannes Gossner, Sammlung gedruckter und ungedruckter Predigten, p. 552 "... a messenger of Christ must be sent by Christ, as he was sent by the Father, must not come running from himself to the Gentiles, not to be driven by people, not by flesh and blood. He has his mission and his calling to prove like Christ in the synagogue of his home town proved his divine mission from the Bible: "The Spirit of the Lord is with me, he therefore has anointed me and sent me to proclaim" (Luke 4:18; Is. 61:1). Whom Christ has not breathed and anointed with the Holy Spirit, shall rest at home. Who is the messenger must be able to call his master ..." (Transl. U.S.).

the Spirit blows where the Spirit wills in ways over which no human being has control (cf. John 3:8)."[260]

Consequently, the task of Christians in their mission is to be sent by God into the world, as witnesses. The active role of his witness, however, is being modified in favour of the divine activity. Man only participates in this. Coming from these two preconditions, codes of conduct for the practice of missionary action are being agreed upon, which cannot be cited here in detail. The dialogue with other religions is explicitly part of this by formulating basic rules of respect:

> "10. Renouncing false witness. Christians are to speak sincerely and respectfully; they are to listen in order to learn about and understand others' beliefs and practices, and are encouraged to acknowledge and appreciate what is true and good in them. Any comment or critical approach should be made in a spirit of mutual respect, making sure not to bear false witness concerning other religions.
>
> 11. Ensuring personal discernment. Christians are to acknowledge that changing one's religion is a decisive step that must be accompanied by sufficient time for adequate reflection and preparation, through a process ensuring full personal freedom."[261]

Furthermore, the "Code of Conduct" calls for the establishment of forums of inter-religious dialogue to support the general welfare.

b) Mission and evangelism in changing landscapes

At the 10th General Assembly of the WCC in Busan in June 2013, a new declaration on "Mission and Evangelism in Changing Landscapes" was presented by the Commission on World Mission and Evangelism. It is the second declaration of the WCC on mission, following the integration of the International Mission Council in New Delhi in 1961.

---

260 Christian Witness in a multi-religious world.

261 A.a.O.

The declaration is theologically voluminous and explicitly takes up the "Code of Conduct".[262] In the basic explanatory part, the term, "mission", is, unlike in the "Code of Conduct", substantially explained. Mission is the participation in the mission of the trinity of God who invites us to fullness of life.[263] Particularly lovely is the perception found in the affirmation closing the declaration: Mission is "an invitation to the feast in the kingdom of God. It is the mission of the church to prepare this feast and to invite everyone to the feast of life."[264] This reminds me of the mission history of the Gossner Church since a common meal communion and the question of social equality in that context triggered the first conversion.[265] This image and the corresponding term of the fullness of life are noticeable, too, because they pick up an eschatological picture: God will produce this meal communion, the feast, and the fullness of life for everyone at the end of the day. This is what we shall be witnesses for at all times and be servants in establishing this future community. Nevertheless, the "landscapes" for this witness and service change in the course of time. Starting from the idea of the fullness of life, the declaration encompasses four subjects, orienting themselves according to these "changing landscapes":

- The ecological question: If in mission man participates in the work of God's spirit and if this is the same spirit of God's creation, then the witness of the fullness of life also includes

---

262 http://www.oikoumene.org/en/resources/documents/wcc-commissions/mission-and-evangelism/together-towards-life-mission-and-evangelism-in-changing-landscapes.html, No. 86-92.

263 Ibid., No. 1: "God invites us into the life-giving mission of the Triune God and empowers us to bear witness to the vision of abundant life for all in the new heaven and earth."

264 Ibid., No. 101: invitation to the "feast in the kingdom of God" (Luke 14:15). The mission of the church is to prepare the banquet and to invite all people to the feast of life.

265 Cf. the Paper "Mission as Misunderstanding - An Observation on Conversion Processes" in this book.

the ecological question. How do we witness the fullness of God in the light of climate change?[266]

- The globalisation: If mission means participating in the fullness of life, then we will have to recognise Jesus turning himself towards the oppressed and marginalised (Luke 4). Although this is an eschatological vision, the participation in God's mission motivates us to fight against and withstand the hostile powers of Mammon.[267] Mission expects specific perspectives on the Gospel by the marginalised themselves[268] and looks critically on the Western churches, who have agreed to an alliance with power and capital.[269]

---

266 Cf. the Paper "Mission as Misunderstanding - An Observation on Conversion Processes" in this book. No. 20: "Mission with creation at its heart is already a positive movement in our churches through campaigns for eco-justice and more sustainable lifestyles and the development of spiritualities that are respectful of the earth. However, we have sometimes forgotten that the whole of creation is included in the reconciled unity towards which we are all called (2 Cor. 5:18-19)."

267 Ibid., No. 43: "Participation in God's ongoing work of liberation and reconciliation by the Holy Spirit, therefore, includes discerning and unmasking the demons that exploit and enslave. For example, this involves deconstructing patriarchal ideologies, upholding the right to self-determination for Indigenous peoples, and challenging the social embeddedness of racism and casteism." No. 45: "and whose love is characterized by mutuality, reciprocity and interdependence. It, therefore, requires a commitment to struggle and resist the powers that obstruct the fullness of life that God wills for all, and a willingness to work with all people involved in movements and initiatives committed to the causes of justice, dignity and life."

268 Ibid., No. 38: "Living on the margins, however, can provide its own lessons. People on the margins have agency, and can often see what, from the centre, is out of view. People on the margins, living in vulnerable positions, often know what exclusionary forces are threatening their survival and can best discern the urgency of their struggles; people in positions of privilege have much to learn from the daily struggles of people living in marginal conditions."

269 Ibid., No. 48: "In reality, however, mission, money and political power are strategic partners. Although our theological and missiological talk says a lot about the mission of the church being in solidarity with the poor, sometimes in practice it is much more concerned with being in the centres of power, eating with the rich and lobbying for money to maintain ecclesial bureaucracy. This

- The Church: The Church is the place where the believers gather in this world. If we understand mission as witness of the fullness of life, the churches must be sending churches. "The church is serving the mission and it glorifies God in self-humbling love." In this sense, priorities of ecclesiastical action must be sought in mission and hospitality.[270]
- Evangelism and inter-religious dialogue: It is in the nature of the Church to witness deliberately the fullness of life to the entire world and to invite the world to repent. In history, this invitation was not always spelled out in the adequate attitude of humbleness of the mission of Jesus. Today, however, it is recognised that God's spirit can be experienced in other religions. In this sense, we have to face other religions with humbleness and respect, as if we face God himself.

Particularly, this latest aspect pursues the concept of the "Code of Conduct" by not only listening to the other perceptions of faith and possibly criticising them but also by joining into an active movement of a common search for the fullness of life. This is particularly encouraged by Luther's concept of the freedom of conscience.[271]

---

poses particular challenges to reflect on what is the good news for people who are privileged and powerful."

270 Ibid., No. 62: "The church is a servant in God's mission and not the master. The missionary church glorifies God in self-emptying love."

271 Ibid., No. 93: "We believe that the Spirit of Life brings joy and fullness of life. God's Spirit, therefore, can be found in all cultures that affirm life. The Holy Spirit works in mysterious ways, and we do not fully understand the workings of the Spirit in other faith traditions. We acknowledge that there is inherent value and wisdom in diverse life-giving spiritualities. Therefore, authentic mission makes the "other" a partner in, not an "object" of mission." No. 94 "Dialogue at the religious level is possible only if we begin with the expectation of meeting God who has preceded us and has been present with people within their own contexts. God is there before we come (Acts 17) and our task is not to bring God along, but to witness to the God who is already there."

2.3. Final considerations – Dialogue as Lutheran identity

The Christian Church has had severe problems with the concept of tolerance. Starting from the concepts of the ancient world – the connection between state and church – an attitude of intolerance against other religions and perceptions of faith became predominant in the established Western denominations. During the Reformation, Martin Luther appealed to the freedom of conscience. In the course of the developments and the untying of the connection between state and church, the Lutheran claim to freedom of faith and conscience was secularised and became part of democratic structures. In the increasingly religiously motivated conflicts of the globalised world, a significant contribution of religions, in terms of dialogic tolerance, can be expected. The signals into this direction are set by world Christianity in the "Code of Conduct" and the declaration "Together Towards Life". In these documents, the tension between the claim of truth of a person's own faith and respect towards the other religion is being solved in an inclusive manner. We perceive the other person as partner in the witness of the fullness of life offered by God to everyone. Lutheran identity contributes one fundamental aspect to this process of dialogic tolerance: Man stands with his conscience and faith in direct relation to God. Whoever believes this for his own faith will have to accept this for others as well and will have to recognise him or her as a creature of God. God wants all humans to participate in their fullness.

Reflection

The area of Chotanagpur has now become a focal point in the church history of India. As Gossner Theological College, we contributed our part, by presenting the work of P. C. Horo under the title ***Christian Missions in Bihar and Jharkhand till 1947,*** which was reedited by Jose Kalapura. Now we are delighted to present the book of Rev. Dr. Ulrich Schoentube with sketches, which not only focuses the history of the Gossner Evangelical Church in Chotanagpur and Assam, but also gives some ecumenical approaches on mission. The collection, for us as a College family, revives the memories of academic sessions of the last seven years, in which several papers were discussed, especially the questions on the development of an Adivasi Theology and the social relevance of the Gospel, connecting inter-alia with the entire theological discussions.

The academic work of the College on these matters had practical consequences on it and also on the identity of Christians in the Chotanagpur area. It was possible with the help of the German Research Foundation and Gossner Mission to collect relevant archive materials from the Central Council Office of Gossner Evangelical Lutheran Church as well from the former Mission Stations at rural areas. The documents are saved in the new central Archive, scanned and available on the Internet together with the sources of Gossner

Mission, Berlin. We are proud to be the first Church in Indian context, which opens the doors for the international research of one part of the history of Christianity in India. The digitized Archive and the recent publications show the academic interest of the Gossner Theological College to deepen the questions of the historical roots of our Christian identity as Adivasis and the cultural transformations of the Gospel towards the development of an Adivasi Theology for the current challenges of our church ministry.

Dr. Manmasih Ekka
Principal, Gossner Theological College

Bibliography

1. Sources

Peter *Abaelard*, Collationes, ed. and transl. by John Marenbon and Giovanni Orlando, Dialogus inter Philosophum Judaeum et Christianum, Oxford 2003.

Aurelius *Augustin*, Tractatus in Johannem, ed. by Philip Schaff, Christian Classics Etheral Library (CCEL), Nicene and Post-Nicene Fathers Series I, Vol. 7. St Augustine: Homilies on the Gospel of John, Edinburgh, http://www.ccel.org/.

Die *Biene* auf dem Missionsfelde, Journal of Gossner Mission since 1834 ("The Bee in the Mission Field" - abbreviated: Biene).

Johannes *Bonaventura*, Commentaria in quattuor Libros sententiarum Magisteri Petri Lombardi, Tert. Lib. Dist. IX, Art. I, qu. II. Opera Omnia, Rom 1892-1902.

Historia J. *Cochlaei* de actis et scripsis M. Lutheri, Köln 1568.

World Missionary *Conference* 1910, Vol. 1-8, London/Toronto 1910.

Cassio Dio, Roman History ed. by Earnest Cary, Loeb Classical Library, 9 volumes, Greek texts and English translation: Harvard 1914 thru 1927.

(http://penelope.uchicago.edu/Thayer/E/Roman/Texts/Cassius_Dio/52*.html).

Otto *Fischer*, Evangelisches Pfarrerbuch für die Mark Brandenburg seit der Reformation, Berlin 1941.

Phillipp *Gercken*: Codex diplomaticus brandenburgensis, V. 7, Stendal 1782.

Johannes Evangelista *Gossner*,

Das Herz des Menschen. Ein Tempel Gottes oder eine Werkstaette des Satans, Berlin 1812. (engl ed.: The Heart of Man. Either a temple of God or the habitation of Satan, Pa 1822).

Sammlung auserlesener Lieder von der erlösenden Liebe, Leipzig 1825.

Choralbuch, Enthaltend die Melodieen zu der Sammlung auserlesener Lieder von der erlösenden Liebe und dem Schatzkaestchen, Leipzig 1825.

Schatzkaestchen enthaltend biblische Betrachtungen mit erbaulichen Liedern auf alle Tage im Jahre zur Beförderung häuslicher Andacht und Gottseligkeit, Leipzig 1825. English Edition: Johannes Gossner, The Spiritual Casket of daily Bible Meditations ... Translated from the German. With an introduction by ... E. H. Bickersteth, London 1864.

Sammlung gedruckter und ungedruckter Predigten, Nürnberg 1838.

Andreas Bodenstein von *Karlstadt*, Von der abthuung der bylder/ vnnd das keyn Betler under den Christen seyn soll, Wittenberg 1522, herausgegeben von Hans Lietzmann, Kleine Texte für theologische und philosophische Vorlesungen und Übungen, Nr.74, Bonn 1911.

Johann Dettloff *Prochnow*, Johannes Gossner. Biographie aus Tagebüchern und Briefen, Erster Theil bis zum Schluß seiner Wirksamkeit in Petersburg, Berlin o.J.; Zweiter Theil bis zu seinem Tode, Berlin 1874.

The *Gossner Mission* Archive, G1-812, Personalakten des Stifters Johannes Evangelista Gossner 1828-1839.

Gossner Mission, Festschrift zum 75-jährigen Bestehen der Gossnerschen Mission, Berlin 1911.

Gregor der Große: Opera Omnia, Migne Patrologia Latina Vol. 77, Paris 1862.

Hans *Lietzmann* (Hg.), Die Wittenberger Ordnung von 1522, Kleine Texte Nr.21, Berlin 1931.

Martin *Luther,*

Werke, Kritische Gesamtausgabe, Weimar 1883-2001, (abbreviated: WA).

Luther Works Vol. 40, Philadelphia 1958.

Martin Leberecht de Wette, Luthers Briefe von seinem Aufenthalt auf der Coburger Veste während des Reichstags zu Augsburg, bis zur Schließung der Wittenberger Konkordie, Vol. 4, Berlin 1824.

Martin Luther, Briefe, Eine Auswahl, herausgegeben von Günter Wartenberg, Leipzig 1983.

Martin Luther, Taschenausgabe, ed. by Horst Beintker et all., Vol. 1-5, Berlin 1981.

Phillip *Melanchthon*, Loci Communes, CR 21, Reprint, New York. 1963.

Apologie der Augsburgischen Konfession, Bekennnisschriften der evangelisch-lutherischen Kirche, herausgegeben im Gedenkjahr der Augsburgischen Konfession 1939, Göttingen 1963 (BSLK), full text is available: http://bocl.org?AP+IV.

Le Miroir de pécheur, 1739-1754, Bibliothèque nationale de France, département Réserve des livres rares, RES P-YE-2510.

Christian Otto *Mylius*: Corpus Constitutionum Marchicarum oder Koeniglich preußische und churfüsrtlich Brandenburgische in Chur und Marck Brandenburg … ergangene Ordungen, edicta, mandata, Berlin/ Halle 1735-55.

Ludwig *Nottrott*: Die Gossnersche Mission unter den Kohls. Bilder aus dem Missionsleben, Halle 1874.

Ludwig *Nottrot*: Die Gossnersche Mission unter den Kohls. Die Arbeiten in den Jahren 1874-1887, Halle 1888.

Heiko Oberman et al., Kirchen und Theologiegeschichte in Quellen, Bd. IV, Vom Konfessionalismus zur Moderne, Neukirchen-Vluyn 1997.

Quintus Aurelius Symmachus, Relatio III, 10, in: Richard Klein Der Streit um den Victoriaaltar. Die dritte Relatio des Symmachus und die Briefe 17, 18 und 57 des Mailänder Bischofs Ambrosius. Wissenschaftliche Buchgesellschaft, Darmstadt 1972, Lat Text: (http://www.hsaugsburg.de/~Harsch/Chronologia/Lspost04/Symmachus/sym_re03.html).

Deutsche *Reichsakten*, Jüngere Reihe Bd. 2, Gotha 1899, reprint Göttingen 1962.

Johann *Salver*, Geistlicher Seelenspiegel, in welchem ein jeder seines Heyls begieriger Christenmensch sich ersehen, den Stand seiner Seelen erkennen und seinen Lebenswandel, zu seinem Heyl nützlich danach einrichten kann, Würzburg 1733, Vd 18 12648582001.

Emil *Sehling*, Die Evangelischen Kirchenordnungen des XVI. Jahrhunderts, Vol. 3, Leipzig 1909.

Theodosius I., Edikt "Cunctos Populos" Theodosius I. Edikt "Cunctos Populos" (Edict of Thessalonica) in: Codex Theodosianus, XVI, 1.2. Clyde Pharr, Theresa Sherrer Davidson, The Theodosian code: a translation, with annotatison, of all source matrial of Roman Law, Nashwille 1945.

Johann Hinrich *Wichern*, Beiblatt der Fliegenden Blätter aus dem Rauhen Hause 10, No. 11 (1859).

Johann Hinrich *Wichern*, Gesammelte Schriften D. Johann Hinrich Wicherns. Briefe und Tagebuchblätter D. Johann Hinrich Wicherns, I. Band 1826-1848, Hamburg 1901.

2. Biographies

Hermann *Dalton*, Johannes Gossner. Ein Lebensbild aus der Kirche des 19. Jahrhunderts, Berlin 1874.

Karl *Foertsch*, Dr. Dettloff Prochnow, Gossners Missionar und Nachfolger, Berlin 1939.

Walter *Holsten*, Johannes Evangelista Gossner. Glaube und Gemeinde, Göttingen 1949.

Karl Friedrich *Ledderhose*, Johann Jänicke, der evangelisch Lutherische Prediger an der böhmischen – oder Bethlehems-Kirche zu Berlin, nach seinem Leben und Wirken, Berlin 1863.

Hans *Lokies*, Johannes Gossner. Ein Bekenner und Diener Jesu Christi. Zeugen des gegenwärtigen Gottes, 2. durchgesehene Auflage, Gießen 1956.

Hans *Luckey*, Gottfried Wilhelm Lehmann und die Entstehung einer deutschen Freikirche, Kassel 1939.

Emma *Poel*, Denkwürdigkeiten aus dem Leben von Amalie Sieveking, in deren Auftrage von einer Freundin derselben verfasst, Hamburg 1860.

Johann Dettloff *Prochnow*, Johannes Evangelista Gossner, nebst Übersicht der Gossnerschen Missionstätigkeit, Berlin 1859.

Charlotte *Sauer*, Fremdling und Bürger, Lebensbild des Johannes Evangelista Gossner, Berlin 1967.

3. Essays and Monographs

Jan *Assmann*, Religion und kulturelles Gedächtnis, München 2000. Jan Assmann Religion and Cultural Memory: Ten Studies (Cultural Memory in the Present) transl. by Rodney Livingstone, Stanford University Press 2006.

Heinrich *Balz*, Der Anfang des Glaubens, Theologie des Glaubens und der jungen Kirchen, Erlangen 2010.

Marsallan *Bage*, Phänomenologie der Munda-Religion, Berlin 1960.

Joseph *Bara*, Unlocking Tribal Knowledge to the World: German Missionaries in Chhotanagpur, East India 1850-1930, in: Ulrich von der Heyden et al., Missionsgeschichte als Geschichte der Globalisierung von Wissen: transkulturelle Wissensaneignung in Afrika und Asien im 17., 18. und 19. Jahrhundert, Berlin 2010, pp. 55-66.

Dieter *Becker*, Den Anderen mit Achtung und Ehrerbietung zugewandt, in: Mission Erfüllt? Edinburgh 1910 – 100 Jahre Weltmission, Jahrbuch Mission 2009, pp. 80-86.

Kwame *Bediako*, Christianity in Africa, The Renewal of a Non-Western Religion, Edinburgh 1995.

Michael *Beintker*, Vom Bekenntniswechsel Johann Sigismunds bis zum Edikt von Potsdam, in: Günther Wirth (Ed.), Berliner Kirchengeschichte, Berlin 1987.

Hellmut *Borutta*, Revolution für das Recht, Erlangen 1994.

Martin *Brecht*, Martin Luther, Vol. 1 Sein Weg zur Reformation 1483-1521, Stuttgart 3rd ed. 1990.

Siegfried *Bräuer*/ Hans-Jürgen Görtz, Art. Thomas Müntzer, in: Martin Greschat, Gestalten der Kirchengeschichte, Vol. 5, pp. 335-352.

Siegfried *Bräuer*: Umgestaltung und Übergänge. Beobachtungen zu den Anfängen des reformatorischen Gottesdienstes, in: Revue d' Histoire et de Philosophie Religieuses, 85 (2005), pp. 51-71.

Peter van der *Coelen*, Bilder aus der Schrift, Studien zur alttestamentlichen Druckgraphik des 16. und 17. Jahrhunderts, Bern 2002.

Peter *Daly*, The Emblem in Early Modern Europe, Contributions to the Theory of Emblem, Ashgate 2014.

Jhakmak Neeraj *Ekka*, Taking to the Efforts of Reinterpretation of the Gospel and Creation of Literature in the Face of the Challenges we have today, in: Ulrich Schoentube, Zwischen Wort und Tat, Beiträge zum 150. Todestag von Johannes Evangelista Gossner, Erlangen 2009, pp. 48-63.

Rolf *Engelsing*, Analphabetentum und Lektüre, Zur Sozialgeschichte des Lesens in Deutschland zwischen feudaler und industrieller Gesellschaft, Stuttgart 1973.

Walter *Elliger*, Die Evangelische Kirche der Union, ihre Vorgeschichte und Geschichte, Witten 1967.

Erich *Foerster*, Die Entstehung der Preußischen Landeskirche unter der Regierung König Friedrich Wilhelms des Dritten nach den Quellen erzählt, Vol. 1, Tübingen 1905.

Paul *Graff*, Geschichte der Auflösung der alten gottesdienstlichen Formen in der evangelischen Kirche Deutschlands bis zum Eintritt der Aufklärung und des Rationalismus, 2 Vol., Göttingen 1921/1939.

Hans-Jürgen *Goertz* H.-J., J. Jaquiery & P. Matheson, Thomas Müntzer apocalyptic mystic and revolutionary, Edinburgh 1993.

Wolfgang *Günther*, Edinburgh 1910 – gemeinsam die Welt für Christus gewinnen, in: Mission Erfüllt? Edinburgh 1910 – 100 Jahre Weltmission, Jahrbuch Mission, 2009, pp 16-23.

Rebekka *Habermas*, Mission im 19. Jahrhundert-Globale Netze des Religiösen, in: Historische Zeitschrift 187 (2008), pp. 629-679.

Rebekka *Habermas*/ Richard Hölzl, Mission Global, Köln 2014.

Andand Sebeyan *Hemrom*, The Needs for Ecumenical Efforts in Mission Activism in the Face of Threats to Adivasi Identity, Survival Existence, in ibid., pp. 64-79.

Adolf *Herte*, Die Lutherbiographie des Johannes Cochläus. Eine quellenkritische Untersuchung, Diss. Münster 1915.

Volker *Herrmann*: Innere Mission und Diakonie bei Johann Hinrich Wichern, in: Ders./ Jürgen Gohde/ Heinz Schmidt (Hg.): Johann Hinrich Wichern – Erbe und Auftrag. Stand und Perspektiven der Forschung, Heidelberg 2007, pp 130-166.

Prem Chand *Horo*, Christian Missions in Bihar and Jharkhand till 1947, ed. by Jose Kalapura, New Delhi 2014.

Thomas *Jellinghaus*, Die Kolhs in Ostindien und ihre Christianisierung, in: Allgemeine Missionszeitschrift (AMZ) 1 (1874), pp. 24-35. 105-111, 167-184, 203-214; 253-270; 290-295, 341-350.

Peter Samuel *Jost*, Karl Hartenstein und die missio Dei, Zeitschrift für Missionswissenschaft, 3-4/ 2010, pp. 305-325.

Christ Sumit Abhay *Kerketta*, Adivasi Theology, Towards a Relevant Christian Theology for the Jharkhand Adivasi, Ranchi 2009.

Justus M. van der *Kroef*, Patterns of Cultural Change in three primitive Societies, in: Social Research Vol. 24. No. 4 (1957), pp. 427-456.

Silke *Leonhard*, Thomas Klie, Schauplatz Religion Grundzüge einer performativen Religionsdidaktik, Leipzig 2003.

Victoria *Luker*, Millenarism in India. The Movement of Birsa Munda, in: Geoffrey A. Oddie, Religious Traditions in South Asia, Interaction and Change, Richmond 1998, pp. 51-64.

S. Matho, Hundred Years of Christian Missions in Chotanagpur since 145, 2nd ed. Patna 1994.

Christian Gotthold *Neudecker*, Die handschriftliche Geschichte Ratzebergers über Luther und seine Zeit, Jena 1850.

Alfred *Nottrott*, Der gegenwärtige Stand der Kols-Mission mit besonderer Berücksichtigung der Landfrage, Allgemeinde Missionszeitschrift (AMZ) 16 (1889), pp. 257-281.

Karl Heinrich Christian *Plath*, Gossners Segensspuren in Nordindien, Eine geschichtliche und missionstheoretische Reisebeschreibung. Friedenau-Berlin: Buchhdlg. d. Gossnerschen Mission 1896.

Sarat Chandra *Roy*, The Mundas and their country, London 1970.

Curt *Schelenz*, Kreis Züllichau Schwiebus, Frankfurt 1970.

Hans J. *Reichhardt*, Die Böhmen in Berlin 1732-1982: eine Ausstellung des Landesarchivs Berlin, 9. Dezember 1982 bis 30. April 1983, Landesarchiv Berlin 1982.

Julius *Richter*, Geschichte der Berliner Missionsgesellschaft 1824-1924, Berlin 1924.

Heinz *Schilling*, Aufbruch und Krise, Deutschland 1517-1648, 4. Ed. Berlin 1998.

Suresh *Singh*, The dust-storm and the hanging mist, Calcutta 1966.

Brain *Stanley*, The World Missionary Conference Edinburgh 1910, Studies in the History of Christian Missions, Grand Rapids, 2009.

Klaus von *Stieglitz*, "Gottes Barmherzigkeit hat noch kein Ende" (Klgl. 3,22). Dank an Vater Gossner, in: Ulrich Schöntube (Hg.):

Zwischen Wort und Tat, Beiträge zum 150. Todestag von Johannes Evangelista Gossner, Erlangen 2009; pp. 156-180.

Margarete Stirm, Bilderfrage in der Reformation, Gütersloh 1977.

Theo *Sundermeyer*, Begegnung mit dem Fremden, Plädoyer für eine verstehende Missionswissenschaft. In: Ders.: Konvivenz und Differenz, Studien zu einer verstehenden Missionswissenschaft. Anlässlich seines 60. Geburtstages herausgegeben von Volker Küster, Erlangen 1995, pp. 76-86.

Theo *Sundermeyer*, Inkulturation als Entäußerung, in: Jan A. B. Jongeneel u.a. Mission and Ecumenism. Essays in Intercultural Theology, Frankfurt/Main 1992, pp. 209-214.

Ernst *Ullmann*, Die Wittenberger Unruhen, Andreas Bodenstein von Karlstadt und die Bilderstürme in Deutschland, in: L'Art et les révolutions, Actes du XXVIIe congrès international d'histoire de l'Art, Bd. 4, 1992, pp. 117-126.

Index

E

F

G

K

L

M

N